A Verse Map of Vancouver

A Verse Map of Vancouver

POETS
(in order of appearance)

Pat Lowther	Trevor Carolan
George Woodcock	Lynda Grace Philippsen
Linda Rogers	Meredith Quartermain
José Emilio Pacheco	Christopher Levenson
Zsuzsi Gartner	Andrea Dancer
Lillian Boraks-Nemetz	Leslie Timmins
Madeline Sonik	John Pass
Tom Wayman	Lionel Kearns
George McWhirter	George Stanley
David Watmough	Christine Schrum
Roy Miki	Bibiana Tomasic
Wes Hartley	Ron Smith
Suzanne Getsinger	Karoly Sandor
Gudrun Will	Mark Cochrane
Fiona Tinwei Lam	Evelyn Lau
Mark Harris	George Fetherling
C.J. Leon	Julia van Gorder
Al Purdy	Shannon Stewart
Daniela Bouneva Elza	Maureen Hynes
Zachariah Wells	Elizabeth Bachinsky
Kate Braid	Diane Sutherland
Stephanie Bolster	Allan Safarik
Gary Geddes	John Donlan
Madeleine Thien	Brian Brett
Rita Wong	Oana Avasilichioaei
William H New	Diane Tucker
Wayne Stedingh	Sandy Shreve
Maxine Gadd	Pam Galloway
Justin Lukyn	David R. Conn
Joseph Ferone	Michael Turner
Maria Sammarco	Kuldip Gill
Bud Osborn	Heidi Greco
Jim Wong-Chu	Joy Kogawa
Jancis M. Andrews	Genni Gunn
Pam Galloway	Diane Sutherland
Daphne Marlatt	Michael Bullock
Barbara Pelman	Renee Norman
Catherine Owen	Daniela Bouneva Elza
Goh Poh Seng	Tana Runyan
Chris Hutchinson	Rob Taylor
George Whipple	Jennica Harper
Russell Thornton	Cameron Johnson
Meredith Quartermain	Anneliese Schultz
Heather Haley	Mavis Jones
Bernice Lever	Laisha Rosnau
Aislinn Hunter	Marita Dachsel

A Verse Map of Vancouver

EDITED BY

George McWhirter

PHOTOGRAPHY BY

Derek von Essen

anvil
PRESS

Anvil Press Publishers Inc.
P.O. Box 3008, Main Post Office
Vancouver, BC V6B 3X5 Canada
www.anvilpress.com

Library and Archives Canada Cataloguing in Publication

    The verse map of Vancouver / edited by George
McWhirter ; photographs by Derek von Essen.

Poems.
ISBN 978-1-897535-02-8

    1. Canadian poetry (English)--21st century.
2. Vancouver (B.C.)--Poetry. 3. Vancouver (B.C.)--
Pictorial works. I. McWhirter, George

PS8287.V35V47 2009   C811'.60803271133   C2009-900864-5

Printed and bound in Canada
Cover & Interior design by Derek von Essen

Represented in Canada by the Literary Press Group
Distributed by the University of Toronto Press

The publisher gratefully acknowledges the financial assistance of the Canada Council for
the Arts, the Book Publishing Industry Development Program (BPIDP), and the Province
of British Columbia through the B.C. Arts Council and the Book Publishing Tax Credit.

THE POET LAUREATE

The Poet Laureate is an honorary two-year position. During his or her term, the Poet Laureate acts as a champion for poetry, language and the arts, and creates a unique artistic legacy through public readings and civic interactions. The Poet Laureate attends a variety of civic functions, participates in public poetry events and carries through one or more special civic projects. The general mandate is to raise the status of poetry in the everyday consciousness of Vancouverites. Each Poet Laureate is free to pursue an individual agenda in addition to their civic duties.

The Poet Laureate Program was made possible by a generous donation from Dr. Yosef Wosk whose significant cultural leadership in Vancouver includes ongoing support for libraries and the literary arts. Dr. Wosk's donation is matched by the BC Arts Renaissance Fund and held in trust by the Vancouver Foundation, which ensures the continuation of the Poet Laureate position.

The Poet Laureate Program is a partnership of the City of Vancouver, the Vancouver Public Library and the Vancouver International Writers & Readers Festival.

Vancouver Public Library

INTRODUCTION

The intent of *A Verse Map of Vancouver* is to represent the city's places and principal features in poetry, not to provide a collection of its most prominent poems or poets. Such anthologies exist — for example, Allan Safarik's city centennial *Vancouver Poetry*, Polestar, 1986. A call went out for poems on Vancouver's streets, parks, beaches, bridges and buildings — if there are omissions, it is because of submissions and perhaps suspicion or apprehension on the part of some poets that *A Verse Map of Vancouver* demanded that the muse serve up, if not poems for specific civic occasions, then forced descriptodes for the city's locations. I am glad so many poets did respond with their word-windows on Vancouver. Inevitably, this anthology will fall short of all possible poems and pictures of Vancouver. It lacks a poem for any of its graveyards, schools or golf courses, but those missing Vancouver places await in other verse maps of the city.

Except for three, all poems are by living contemporaries and lie within Vancouver city boundaries. All the poets, however, do not dwell within these; other cities and countries have residential claim on their talent. Cut off at the wrist by Boundary Road, with finger and thumb peninsulas of Point Grey (bounded by the Fraser River and Strait of Georgia) and West End-Stanley Park (by False Creek, English Bay and Burrard Inlet), the layout of Vancouver is "just so damned rational," as Mark Harris puts it: avenues that run East to West are monotonously numbered, and the streets that stretch North to South, named. As to its layout, if the plotting of this book were rendered in a treasure hunt or The Amazing Race's cryptic instructions, it would go: *1) Start at the cherry trees and young girls on horses near the Fraser River, then follow the water to Railroad Station No.1. 2) Go to Railroad Station No. 2, set off from the angel, move east, almost as far as you can go in Vancouver proper. 3) Return to Railroad Station No. 2, from the SeaBus, head south and south-west through city centre to the crosstown, 99 B-Line bus*, get on, and so on, to earn a reward in every situation. *Verse Map* returns to the Yaletown quayside, circuiting the water a second time to the Second Narrows Bridge and Vancouver-Burnaby boundary before venturing back to Mt. Pleasant, Little Mountain, Shaughnessy, the South Slope and Marpole, ending at the airport across the river from where it started.

I would like to thank Brian Kaufman of Anvil Press for undertaking such a large venture in verse, Derek von Essen for putting a year into the photographs for this book, and Yosef Wosk, whose endowment to create the Vancouver Poet Laureateship inspired the Vancouver Foundation to invest the matching project monies that made Derek von Essen's work possible. Paul Whitney, Vancouver's City Librarian, and the Central Library staff, Hal Wake, the Director, and crew at the Vancouver International Writers & Readers Festival are to be thanked for their support and resources. I would also like to thank the City of Vancouver's Office of Cultural Affairs, especially Marnie Rice (our minder), for her assistance, the Chief of External Relations and Protocol, Sven Buemann, for early help in the anthology's format, and finally, Mayor Gregor Robertson and Vancouver City Council, for adopting *A Verse Map of Vancouver* as a gift for distinguished visitors. I hope many will visit both the book and the city.

– George McWhirter, Vancouver, March 2009

CONTENTS

PAGE

The Poet Laureate 3

Introduction 5

Vancity Pat Lowther 8

The cherry tree on Cherry Street George Woodcock 10

Everything but horses Linda Rogers 12

Musqueam José Emilio Pacheco 14

Wreck(ed) Beach, 1997 Zsuzsi Gartner 16

A kiss in Nitobe Garden Lillian Boraks-Nemetz 18

Gage Tower Madeline Sonik 20

Sea wrack (excerpt) Tom Wayman 22

Where Kits sits George McWhirter 24

Kits Pool David Watmough 26

There are some days Roy Miki 28

Kitsilano Point ghost muskrat swamp... Wes Hartley 30

Kitsilano is not Nantucket... Jennifer S. Getsinger 32

Date stamp Gudrun Will 34

Vanier Park Fiona Tinwei Lam 36

The town is just so damned rational Mark Harris 38

Gulls (Granville Island); Seal at English Bay C.J. Leon 40

Piling blood Al Purdy 42

A walk down apostrophe lane... Daniela Bouneva Elza 44

Leg in Boot Square Zachariah Wells 46

Union welders: overtime Kate Braid 48

Terminal Stephanie Bolster 50

Active trading Gary Geddes 52

SkyTrain: Main and Terminal, 1983 Madeleine Thien 54

take a st. and Rita Wong 56

my Vancouver starts William H. New 58

4:00 a.m. Wayne Stedingh 60

The new Old Spaghetti Factory... Maxine Gadd 62

002864 Justin Lukyn 64

BC Collateral Joseph Ferone 66

Meals on Wheels, nineteen eighty-eight Maria Sammarco 68

Jackson avenue and *east* hastings Bud Osborn 70

pender street east; curtain of rain Jim Wong-Chu 72

Grandmothers in Chinatown Jancis M. Andrews 74

Sun Yat-Sen's garden Pam Galloway 76

moonshine Daphne Marlatt 78

Sam's Shirt Shop on Hastings Barbara Pelman 80

Alleyway, 8 a.m. Catherine Owen 82

Evening on Victoria Goh Poh Seng 84

The man who lives in the gazebo Chris Hutchinson 86

SeaBus George Whipple 88

When the big hand is on the starfish Russell Thornton 90

Cathedral Meredith Quartermain 92

Whore in the eddy Heather Haley 94

Words on the streets Bernice Lever 96

Under Christchurch bells Aislinn Hunter 98

What Jack Shadbolt said Trevor Carolan 100

Happy Hour: Bacchus Lounge Lynda Grace Philippsen 102

Scaffolding Meredith Quartermain 104

Listening in Christopher Levenson 106

Erasure at Westcoast Tattoo Andrea Dancer 108

Where the numbers meet the trees Leslie Timmins 110

The crosstown bus John Pass 112

Vancouver General Lionel Kearns 114

Fire alarm George Stanley 116

Purgatory Christine Schrum 118

99 Express — 8 a.m. Bibiana Tomasic 120

The fourth moon of Broadway Ron Smith 122

Quinte (Goddess on Tenth Avenue) Karoly Sandor 124

Point Grey, Saturday paper Mark Cochrane 126

Quayside Evelyn Lau 128

The Sylvia George Fetherling 130

Seawall Stanley Park; The poet... Julia van Gorder 132

December aquarium Shannon Stewart 134

Heronry Maureen Hynes 136

On the death of the Lions Gate... Elizabeth Bachinsky 138

Silver thaw Diane Sutherland 140

Fish candy Allan Safarik 142

Babies' Cottage John Donlan 144

The crabs under the Second Narrows... Brian Brett 146

Museum Oana Avasilichioaei 148

The crows cope Diane Tucker 150

Neighbours (on Marshall Street) Sandy Shreve 152

El Dorado: Champlain Heights Pam Galloway 154

Ridgeway: commuting on two wheels David R. Conn 156

1 a.m. this road, this way Michael Turner 158

...Punjabi Market Kuldip Gill 160

Gravity of the situation: stuck... Heidi Greco 162

happy birthday dear house Joy Kogawa 164

Sestina for Shaughnessy Genni Gunn 166

Across the street Diane Sutherland 168

Autumn, VanDusen Gardens... Michael Bullock 170

57th and Oak Renee Norman 172

grey on grey (a view from... Daniela Bouneva Elza 174

Black Dog survives Tana Runyan 176

Little Mountain Lionel Kearns 178

Down one at The Nat Rob Taylor 180

Nights above Fraser Street Jennica Harper 182

Harriet Street Cameron Johnson 184

Pacific Spirit Park Anneliese Schultz 186

Maple Grove Park Mavis Jones 188

Then: map of the city Laisha Rosnau 190

Airport music Marita Dachsel 192

Acknowledgements 195

Contributors 197

Vancity

PAT LOWTHER

As though you had found a city, dear wanderer,
Lost in the black of a moonless night rim world,
A long-dead city, accustomed to silence,
Intimate sifting of dust and remoteness of dark sea waves.
As though you had come lighting candles in all of the windows,
See how the city shines like the core of love!
See such a blaze of lights above the ghostly sea!
So did you find my dark, ghost-ridden heart and so leave it lighted.

The cherry tree on Cherry Street

GEORGE WOODCOCK

We saw you first as a cloud
fettered to a tree
whose huge gnarled branches draped
a long-lived wooden house.

We saw the house and tree,
its grey against your white.
We bought the house and you
continued to inhabit
your root-filled habitat.

The rooms were servant small,
the ceilings falling, the
paper dropping off walls,
the basement an anthropologist's
agglomeration. Horse furniture,
old spades, the walls insulated
with newspapers whose readers
were long dead. The place's history.

This was the first land settled,
Vancouver 1862, unnamed but months
before Jack Deighton loaded
his canoe with whisky.
The Irish McCleerys, disaffected
Sam and Fitzgerald,
built their homes
on the escarpment.
This was a hired man's hut,
embellished by generations of
Gothicizing carpenters. And
here they planted their great orchard
and called it Cherry Street.

Everything but horses

LINDA ROGERS

In those days, trees grew everywhere, and girls like us tore into the forest, ripping our dresses on huckleberry branches and blackberry thorns when we ran away from the new suburbs, and boys with their pants down around their ankles — everything but horses. On the Fraser flats, we stalked Sunday school stallions that galloped out of the Book of Revelation, tempting them with Eve's aphrodisiac apples because their foamy withers smelled like the pastures that grew in the mud from the mighty river and their noses were as soft as cottonwood seeds that fell like snow where eagles attacked infant seagulls in battles that filled the murdered silence with down.

On the southlands, we rode bareback, and knew the pleasure of girls who love horses.

Faster, we said to the ponies cantering backwards to the time my great-grandmother stopped on her journey to China to deliver the first boy born in the new city of hope, to the moment my grandfather, who'd sung in the trenches, wore a skirt home from the war that ruined his lungs, to the place in the woods where Dzunukwa, Wild Woman, with her pendulous breasts and hairy body, gathered children in her cedar root basket and took them to the other end of the world, away from "what comes next," where girls and ancient forests are safe.

Musqueam

JOSÉ EMILIO PACHECO

The forest facing the sea
   An eagle high up
on the top of a conifer
   It was dusk
On Vancouver Island
   the sun sank

Perhaps it was the Aztlán of the Mexicans

From there seven tribes set out
   and one
founded the Aztec empire

Of Aztlán only certain names remain
   planted along the coast like stones

The eagle was discovered in the bush
   not heraldic
not blazing with light in the dusk
   Decomposing

It preyed on fish
   poisoned by pesticide   garbage
industrial waste

Eagles cruise over Vancouver
   while the people
watch leviathans of iron on the beach

The Aztecs believed that night
   upon night the Sun God
died into the form of an eagle
   and journeyed through the Land of the Dead
to reascend the second day
   (fortified with human blood)
like a jaguar into the centre of the sky

The Vancouver Indians live
   on the Musqueam Reserve
where the Fraser River spills fresh water
   from the mountains into the sea
then spreads wing into the long plumage of waves

The Georgia Strait joins and separates
   Aztlán from solid ground
the Aztec paradise which is extinct
   like Tenochtitlán
city at the umbilicus of the moon

On the Musqueam Reserve
   there are three golf courses
The old lords of the earth
   caddie the sports utensils
of sea monsters

The eagle spirals down
   and the jaguar
has it drained the blood of night?

Wreck(ed) Beach, 1997

ZSUZSI GARTNER

The children at the school for the deaf are the first to sense something's happening. Out in the playground they all stiffen for several seconds, even the girl hanging upside down on the monkey bars, her braids dragging in the sand. Then they start signing rapidly, little fingers fluttering, small fists smacking into palms. The birds rise up and darken the sky all over the city. Somewhere, someone, thinks the word *Smote*.

Carnivores and lacto-vegans cling to each other as tectonic plates shift and groan beneath them. Chum salmon leap through the massive cracks in the concrete at the foot of the Cambie Street Bridge, chum that haven't been seen here since the 1920s, chum the size of raccoons and grinning like gargoyles.

The ocean spits deadheads, sending logs rocketing through the city like battering rams to crack open the Roman walls of the new library, The Bay, GM Place, St. Paul's Hospital, splitting heads as they whistle by like heat-seeking missiles. All over the city film sets collapse as the earth heaves.

The naked scramble madly up the cliff face from their beach, clutching at branches and swollen arbutus roots, brambles tearing at their pubic hair and genitals, as the ocean roars behind them, a towering inferno of water swallowing pan pipes, arthritic dogs, coolers of dope and sangrias.

They're shocked, not because the end has come, but because it's so New Testament when they had thought it would be man-made — a cold, clinical apocalypse, so they could say *We told you so*.

There's no longer a cliff and we're clutching at air.

A kiss in Nitobe Garden

LILLIAN BORAKS-NEMETZ

How I kissed you that night
in the Japanese garden where we sat
framed in cherry blossom
and bamboo

even time got tangled
in its own twilight foliage
only the leap of a fish
marked the hour
whose scaly finger ordained
our separation

Last night
when I went back to Nitobe
there we were
against the twilight canvas
framed in cherry blossom
and bamboo

and I remembered
how I kissed you
that night

Gage Tower

MADELINE SONIK

Curtains twirl like jigging skirts
out of window hollows

beneath the stairs
bikes pour through the air

and spin
like campus swallows

grey-eyed clouds
race open-mouthed

and paint
the pavement's lustre

leaf bugs
in the throes of love

lift off
with every bluster.

Sea wrack (excerpt)

TOM WAYMAN

1.

The chairs float in
one behind the other
each trailed by the shadow of a wave

Most bob upside down
legs pointed at the grey overcast
low clouds masking the mountains

The chairs are draped
by ribbons of spongy yellow bubbles
ropes of seaslime

or kelp's brown whips and scalloped leaves
Where the furniture grounds against the beach
of gravel and crushed shell

they float in a dirty spume
of discarded bleach bottles
chunks of Styrofoam, wood chips

"Poseidon's Thrones," the locals term the chairs
each time a gale
sends another flotilla ashore

2.

On an ebb tide, beachwalkers
muffled in hooded rain gear
against the misty day

encounter almost every month
a finished wood staircase
with risers and banisters intact

though streaked with water stains
and barnacled
Above the drenched construction

crows and gulls circle, commenting
or settle momentarily alongside
or on it, as though a sea lion carcass

had been washed in
to lie half-coated by sand
The stairs are too ornate

to be maritime
"A mansion must have drowned someplace"
is the neighbourhood wisdom.

Where Kits sits

GEORGE MCWHIRTER

down wide Waterloo,
there is water. Two
waters in its name,
the English/French
water/l'eau
meaning the same
makes it a double
broad boulevard
to the boats.
Always a bow
or a prow —
crude oxidized cliff
of a freighter,
or gay white cruise
ship — at the bottom.
The space of its name
amplified by the nearby
narrowness of Blenheim
and Trafalgar.
As if the streets
matched the margin
or nature
of those victories: Blenheim
goes on and on
to the great Fraser River;
Waterloo gets cut off
by an embankment at 16th
Avenue. Closer
to the water, the fusiliers
camouflaged
in its horse chestnuts
pop
periodic rounds
of fat, barbed green
buckshot,
at the inhabitants,
who have lived and died
in the house to house advance
of wood, stucco and brick,
where a great war is won
every day for the water
view.

Kits Pool

DAVID WATMOUGH

In early days we used to hang around the sunny, shallow end,
But raucous kids dropped ice cream cones, turned water into froth.
    Instant exuberance made a moat between the rest and them,
For youth, the thrill of poolside fun washes away all loss.

    For many years the middle section claimed our hearts.
Here oiled and swollen bellies dithered between shade and sunny gleam.
    Executives swam numerous lengths with grimmest grace.
Academics in dark glasses told acerbic jokes and glowed their self-esteem.

    Eventually came acceptance of the far end of the pool,
Where all is quieter — with stark gaps between the withered pairs.
    Some bony bodies lie stiff-stretched upon *chaiselongues*.
Some guarded talk of missing friends, salubrious poolside air.

But no-one wanting to look down, into those blue depths clear,
    No-one prepared to make that final plunge: frozen in fear.

There are some days

ROY MIKI

You think you won't
Write another poem

You are sitting on the garden
Bench looking at blossoms
On the climbing vine

Kick the metrical
foot in the sand

A small creature lands on the
Armrest an inch from your wrist
And you realize you don't have
A name for the space it occupies
And it appears to psych out
Antennae waving in the still air

Don't let it wrench
one more joint out

Or you are walking along the beach
On an early weekday afternoon and
Pause over a railing to watch the kids
Building castles on an oasis of sand

And you see your reflection in the cloud
Formations to the northwest and bodies
Lie or otherwise move sitting on benches
Reading books and little kids in buggies
Are throwing teethers on the ground

Its hot sand labile
preys on its foraging

And everyone is smiling and others are
Sauntering past lost in frothy thoughts

Why bother to sit down or even expend
The passing seconds thinking of a line
Or even an image to catch your fancy
To wile away the diversionary tactics that
Have come to roost in the daily hassle of
Mediated relationships with the news

How do you recognize
a branch otherwise

Viz that Microsoft has finally caught up with
Dick Tracy with a plastic watch that gives
The most important things one can need

The weather stocks news shoots a glance
At headlines on TV channels lotteries to gamble
Away time sports scores daily diversions (word
Of the day) calendar of dates messages (from
Chosen parties) and horoscopes on loan

"This is going to appeal to techies, early adopters"
Says Eddie Chan, and according to Chris Schneider,
"It's not designed as a productivity device," which is
(You're sure) a relief for poets who might be tempted
To camouflage their trade secrets or otherwise
Abandon efforts to retrieve the river flow of time

Judith Butler writes, "I have moved … perhaps too
Blithely among speculations on the body as the site
Of a common human vulnerability, even as i have
Insisted that this vulnerability is always articulated
Differently, that it cannot be properly thought of outside
A differentiated field of power and, specifically, the
Differentiated operation of norms of recognition."

O ruthless cellular fountains
spraying in far mountains

Who would want to disturb norms of recognition
With stock poetic devices that only remind you
All about the airwaves circulating with such
Nonchalance in the traffic as it moves along
Kits Beach across the vast network of exchanges
(Corporeal and corporate the market guru says
Terror marks the rise and fall of stocks the lingo
Of the free fall into the maelstrom of fortune's arms

Kitsilano Point
ghost muskrat swamp
our home's on native land

WES HARTLEY

August Jack Khahtsahlano told Major Matthews
Kits Point used to be a sprawling muskrat swamp
black willows hardhack cattails heron nest trees
from Snauq longhouse where Burrard Bridge abutment sits
across to Skwayoos summer fishing campground on the beach

A salmon stream ran downhill under Cypress Street
curved west at Cornwall and crossed the tree streets
Walnut Maple Laburnum and Arbutus into English Bay
at Kits Beach bathhouse, Skwayoos campsite
where beachcombers still find arrowheads in the gravel
The CPR dumped thirteen feet of sand in the creekbed
at Maple Street when the railroad tracks were laid down
trucked in fill to the swamp when the streetgrid was laid out
disappeared salmon run, disappeared muskrat swamp
Molson built the brewery on top of Snauq Graveyard

Kitsilano is not Nantucket, though

JENNIFER S. GETSINGER

This is not Nantucket, though
the saltchuck is as cold and unforgiving,
and careless glaciers once discarded stones
that pepper the sandy beach with gravel.
No open ocean but mountain fjords
meet our seaward gaze across the straits.
In the bay, big black ships wait anchored
for berths in port, to load up on resources.
As I swim back and forth across the cove
six cruise ships leave harbour for Alaska.
Then I go home to pace the widow's walk
still hoping some ship's captain yearns for me.

This is not Nantucket, though
iron sperm whale weathervanes
top small but well-appointed homes.
The yacht club serves clam chowder
made from geoducks not quahogs,
while immigrants fish smelt with nets.
Tourists crowd the bed & breakfasts
and writers "watch the pass" from Starbucks.
On each coast a former Concord school girl
tosses poems out to sea in bottles.
Our words reach across the continent
to prove our truths are seaworthy.

Date stamp

GUDRUN WILL

At the corner of MacKenzie and 13th in Kitsilano, the date 1928 is imprinted in the sidewalk cement. Our house down the block is two years older; presumably, construction of civilized footpaths is the finishing touch to a newly carved-out neighbourhood. Every time we step past this little time capsule, we note the remaining houses from that era, consider the patched and battered slab construction of the road, and try to imagine life eight decades ago.

Our moss-filled impression is hardly unique. Throughout the city, dates and street names have been eternalized in the pavement, a practice that goes back to 1906. These markers are mementos of civic history in a medium further altered by cracks, tree roots, and indelible footprints and graffiti. To this day, Vancouver's road crews leave such souvenirs in new sidewalks.

Pedestrians may also occasionally spot capital Ds and Ss from earlier times, indicating that drains and sewers lurked below. Particularly observant ones may also find traces of a contractor's stamp, and may be able to make out the name G. W. Ledingham. It's unclear whether George William came up with the idea himself, but the practice began when he started working for the city.

As today's city workers replace stretches of old sidewalk, they are often careful to cut around the old impressions — a quiet and respectful act of preservation. It would be intriguing to return 100 years from now to muse on scarred and buckled paths laid way back in 2007. Who knows? They might just be the only remaining features of today's streetscapes.

Vanier Park

FIONA TINWEI LAM

He runs into the wind —
the kite rises. Swerves
against it — the kite dives.
Soon, the park is
festooned with colour:
streamers, planes, butterflies.
He runs on amid zig-zags
of sprinting children,
dragging it along the battered grass
until moribund bird
becomes stubborn dog.
For a few metres, it whoops up
like a miracle, then
plummets. We try again.

A year ago, buffeted by wind,
he stood, aged four,
on a mound of sand and logs
by the beach. How he brimmed
sky and sunlight, first kite
soaring.

How I want that back.
Despite my warnings, he runs
between two gnarled trees,
wind behind him. The kite
sags, then snags.
I sigh, lecture, berate,
tug the kite one way, then the other,
finally break the string,
tangling both of us up
in that twisted, blunted tree.

He crouches pondside,
all glory flatlined.
One more time, I say.
He won't hear me.
My son and I, grounded
beneath vacant skies.

The town is just so damned rational

MARK HARRIS

with the exception of Kingsway
(the purpose of which no philosopher
can truly decipher, just as no cartographer
can properly map), all else
makes perfect sense.

This is no Toronto
where the numbering system changes
every quarter kilometre; in Vancouver,
if you know an address, street names
are irrelevant; digits alone
will point you in the right direction.

That's why we need madness
so badly. Who doesn't sigh
with relief while confirming
that the bus stop bench at Third
and Arbutus is still there, eternally awaiting
a public conveyance that will never arrive
and that the quay for a foot ferry
actually floats
over a False Creek…
like the high-rise glimmer of Vancouver,
she's the kind of beauty
you can't do anything with;
she's like a sunset that gives off
neither heat nor light;
she's like a picture that belongs
in neither a museum nor a private home;
like the girl who sits
on that Granville Island ferry,
immured in her own beauty
like a saint in her tomb.

Gulls (Granville Island)

C.J. LEON

Grey as the bay,
with its grey-soup waters pressed
to its grey-wash sky at who-knows-where
in all this homogeneity,

they watch, the gulls,
lock-kneed, mute, twitching their heads
at the provocation of a water-droplet
or to keep loose metre.

They are pensive,
sentinels, not peaceful, thinking it better
to stay low, webs installed on pier or rock,
yawning through the hours,

collecting mizzle,
and shuddering a tail once in a long while
to shake it from them, which is all they get to
this interminable day.

Seal at English Bay

C.J. LEON

Now take that tough-skinned peppered seal out there
with his belly stretched on that mussel-scabbed rock,
swollen like a giant whiskery sweet potato,
carrying the sunshine on his back:

never shaved once his whole CV,
does boat-asana like a natural,
turns his doggie head to scope me out,
and isn't much impressed with what he sees;

and I've never seen the chap before,
and I'm only going from the ready-given,
but he seems to be doing just fine for himself
what with living mammalian life at sea.

Piling blood

AL PURDY

It was powdered blood
in heavy brown paper bags
supposed to be strong enough
to prevent the stuff from escaping
but didn't

We piled it ten feet high
right to the shed roof
working at Arrow Transfer
on Granville Island
The bags weighed 75 pounds
and you had to stand on two
of the bags to pile the top rows
I was six feet three inches
and needed all of it

I forgot to say
the blood was cattle blood
horses sheep and cows
to be used for fertilizer
the foreman said
It was a matter of some delicacy
to plop the bags down softly
as if you were piling dynamite
if you weren't gentle
the stuff would belly out
from bags in brown clouds
settle on your sweating face
cover hands and arms
enter ears and nose
seep inside pants and shirt
reverting back to liquid blood
and you looked like
you'd been scalped
by a tribe of
particularly unfriendly
Indians and forgot to die

We piled glass as well
it came in wooden crates
two of us hoicking them
off trucks into warehouses
every crate
weighing 200 pounds
By late afternoon
my muscles would twitch and throb
in a death-like rhythm
from hundreds of bags of blood
and hundreds of crates of glass

a walk down apostrophe lane
(Sawyer's Lane, False Creek)

DANIELA BOUNEVA ELZA

there was no doubt of an apostrophe
that is   until last monday   when you threw

epistemological uncertainty   in the very name of the place
I claim to live in. with an off the cuff   simple observation.

I surely had seen it before. the sign   at the end of my street.
had I chosen to ignore it?   did I start this chain reaction?

I send an apostrophe   out   into the world
it comes back to me — a convenient echo confirming possession

affirming place of dwelling   re-affirming a permanence that is
too comforting to question.   so   seeking existential security

I went after (what at first sight now seemed) a chimeric apostrophe.

the street sign didn't have one.   my neighbours (in friendly chats)
expressed their confusion. is there   or is there not an apostrophe?

they shared ways they have managed to cope with this uncertainty.
they used it   then they stopped using it after they noticed the sign

at the end of the street.   I felt dispossessed   of a logos I had
embodied and reproduced over and   over numinous times.

constantly got in the mail   the echo of confirmation.
checking the co-op books   and its maps of the enclaves was no help:

it all pointed to a missing punctuation   for the possessive.
after the nagging feeling for a few days   I could not bear it anymore.

I had to know.   I stopped by the post office
checked the zipcode book. (it is a big book).   and there it was

SAWYER'S LANE.   so it was not   *that* imagined.
now   do I take   *their* word   for it?

Leg in Boot Square

ZACHARIAH WELLS

So much reflected, so much exposed, in façades
Of glass ringing this cobbled courtyard
Built on fill. This Creek not merely False,
But dammed, dyked, walled,
Cranes opposite intent on concrete erector
Sets, booms indexed to a boom in the sector,
Also false, fuelled by empty
Specs and green dreams of Olympian
Gold.
     Once, rats scrabbled in the rattle-trap shacks
And sheds they shared with schizo skids and whacked-
Out addicts.
     And once, a limb washed
Ashore, saltchuck sloshing
In the boot it still wore, unclaimed
By any owner.
     Cute? No. This place is maimed.

Union welders: overtime

KATE BRAID
for Sandy Shreve

My brothers are building a dome
of crazed bars jutting
stiff into Expo air.

I watch them at night
hundreds of feet off the ground
magnificently poised
up where the air is clear.
As they work they are stars to me
shooting novas as they strike their arcs,
set welding rods
and build.

That's not welders, my son explains,
sixteen and wise.
Those are lights, set to flash.
Construction is finished,
done.

That night the dome is joyless to me.
I see builders no more,
just the built
ugly attempt
to mimic heaven.

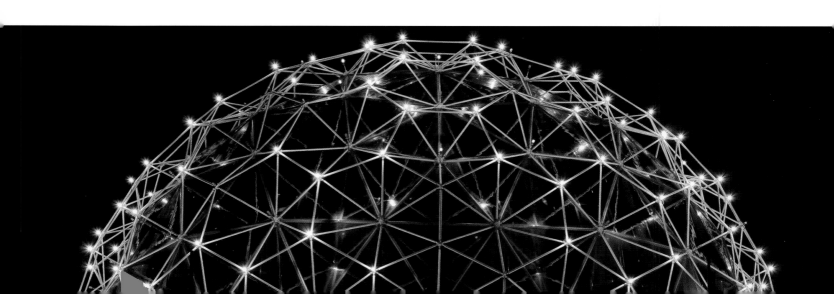

Terminal

STEPHANIE BOLSTER

Where the twin Paulownia bloom
Where we sat on benches, awaiting elsewhere
Where we sat after Main from Broadway
after Main from Hastings
after slippers, ginger, pork belly, glass goldfish paperweights

Where we passed, aloft, on our way
to a day of downtown wanders
or the Seawall or going nowhere
but home

Where Terminal Avenue
Where the Viaduct
Where the SkyTrain platform hovers
and the silver globe

Here it begins
For the rare who come by train
For the cramped who come by bus

Here I arrived from Banff
fresh in love and ready now to leave
this place I'd loved each day
and loved still more
as I dragged my bags
into that mossy evening air

Here I arrived from the rest of the country,
having crossed from Central to Pacific
from where I now call home
to where I still call home
neon flickering on, spring
Paulownia abloom with violet sugar

Here it began and begins
Where we parked the car
those long-shadowed evenings of Expo
when this city was the world

Active trading

GARY GEDDES

I come by my taste for disaster
naturally, raised in a neighbourhood
with streets called Commercial Drive,
Broadway, Terminal Avenue

(money, showbiz, death, the secular
trinity). Weekends and after school
I watch sundry wrecks jockeyed
around the sheet-metal enclosure

at Clark and Hastings, an urban
graveyard for crushed Fords
and devastated Chevies, equal
at last in their demise. The cranes,

meticulous, hoist an Edsel, a species
endangered on the drawing-board,
but consigned here to the privilege
of restoration shed. I study

a torpedo-nosed Studebaker,
totalled in a four-car spectacular
on the Trans-Canada. Up close
the telltale signs: brown stains

on the dash and upholstery; a mute
predictable doll, false eyelashes
feigning sleep. Thus I evolve,
celebrant of the car-crash,

contemplate bruised paint-jobs
under lamplight; the wall
of reflecting hubcaps a constellation
of stars and minor planets; racks

of bumpers, grills, Crusaders' armour.
I'm the Perfect Cold Warrior, ready
for anything — earthquake, Armageddon,
Social Credit. The world's my

gritty oyster. Will it be insurance
or commodities? My pulsing proboscis
picks up advance signals
of the latest bridge collapse

hours before my father — diving-suit,
acetylene torch — is recruited
to cut bodies from the Lego
of twisted girders. Language,

my stock in trade, replete with clues:
landslide, write-off, head-on, impending.
I align myself with Cassandra,
Suzuki, McNeil-Lehrer, I. F. Stone.

Believing the clan loves calamity,
I come running with the latest bad news
only to be rebuked and set upon
outside the city gates.

SkyTrain: Main and Terminal, 1983

MADELEINE THIEN

It's my father who buys the tickets
pockets them as we step into the new-fangled car,
which has blue-and-red racing stripes, emergency buttons
and doors that sigh closed
like my grandfather when he's tired.
When the train starts moving, I suspect
someone's shoving us from behind
and it's all for show because the tracks aren't done
but as my father says, "The future's here" —
light rail, shiny stations, cage doors blinking open,
red boxes spitting tickets — the end of distance,
only seconds between us and the future
for the rest of our days in this wavering city.
Another train will scoop, throw me up against strangers,
set me down, staring at you. Are you staring at me
or the woman I saw on the platform
weeping her old life away, tracing and re-tracing flight,
waving our passes at the wide-armed bridges, eyes open
in the underground, thinking of mothers who kept to their day-in
day-out, till-I-die cars, who sleep now below Patterson Station,
where the graves run down to the river and look up at the rails?
All the bright windows can't keep me here,
there's a red button beside the door
and new lines, built yesterday or still on paper,
stretching the seconds back into our distances before.
Don't leave, leave so that we pour back
like wives and orphaned children.
I find our tickets, years later,
marking the page in the unwritten schedule,
the time stamp informing me that I can't remember
all the places we waited and the things we heard.
It's just that first time that never fades,
my family beside me over Second Avenue, beside me
to the sudden emptiness where the track ran out
and left us suspended like lifting birds
until the moment came to shoot backwards
through the industrious, high-speed
red and blue, yesterday's caboose.

take a st. and

RITA WONG

smell waste
at the corner of 5th and st. george

smell water
gurgling under the manhole covers

corner where the hydrant bursts
water shoots exuberant into sky
hear here

coincidence, haunting, or the stubborn stream's refusal to be confined?

one of 57 former salmon streams on the old map
what's lost may not be the streams but the people
when they try to control the stream's knowledge

re-pair tributary with daylight
twin riparian zone with home

detourne st. george into dan george
Geswanouth Slahoot's spirit knows these unceded streets, snauq

do we?

my Vancouver starts

WILLIAM H. NEW

my vancouver starts somewhere behind blackout curtains,
starts in a fenced-in garden
with the canopy cloth on a wooden toy army truck,
camouflaged,

starts with a streetcar ride
and the dead soldier on cordova street,
limp on an angel's arm,
dragged upward
beside the southeast corner
of the cpr station:

the soldier never moved:

every childhood trip to town, there he stayed, hanging:
heaven as close as maybe
the north shore mountains,
out of reach,
the coastline dissolving in war and death,
as clear as fear and rain

4:00 a.m.

WAYNE STEDINGH

The Gastown clubs close
the young march out casually dressed in camouflage
and the air is a minefield of silences exploding
fuck you and *fuck you*

Four floors above Cordova Street
I turn out the lights inside
the better to see my way into the dark

The young women stand by their reproach
they have kissed the dead
and want their money back

The young men are rain falling in
a torn place in the night
that knocks at a mirror
but is not heard

And on my desk I see my daughter
in a photograph in the dark
her name changed and smiling
concealing the scream of a butterfly

Where will I go now to look for me

I light the black candle inside,
like a man whose eyes have been
wedged out like grapes on a heath
leaving him with one seeing

that a cross-eyed mackerel frozen
and wrapped in a newspaper on my kitchen counter
thaws out only enough to read all the headlines
announcing his obituary

And I turn like a mirror on a string
a whirling Dervish
finding loss has more directions than I

The new Old Spaghetti Factory (Gastown, 53 Water St.)

MAXINE GADD

stay in iambic, don't wail
the boxcars are scorpios, leos, tauruses
and the meaning of this dry mist under the fullest winter sun we have ever
seen is that these systems we have devised to limit our joy are superfluous

i wish you limited yourself cunningly, out of a hunger planets have
for all that leaps from them
or touches the skirts of that personal illumination
a spiral or an island nebula

i sit here in the factory and imagine that's what you do, crazy in huge rings i cast
i sit here caught in the rings i can't cast, watching you become crystal

the boxcars meet St. George somewhere about Blue River where Prospero hides
cunning amid birch and lavender
Indians are sparring in Pigeon Park

near Honest John's a man not defined by any occupation laughs at my friend
who has a headache: "Yr beauty
lines me up, like one of those singers."

the things i
shld not have noticed
i wrack my eyes to see below
what was so easily pleasant
the waitress asking you if you play golf

and
THE BIG GRINGO
DROPPING SILVER
onto the sidewalk

002864

JUSTIN LUKYN

Taking one last look at the pole, he sees, nailed in at eye level, a kind of metal credit card. Looking down the alley, all the poles have them. Of no interest to him and perhaps not to you either, these yellow metal cards tell electricians in the extraordinarily dull terms of longitude and latitude their precise position on the earth.

Trying to pry the card loose of its nails and badly bending the metal, Henry Pepper pockets the thing to suffer a week's worth of burdensome Nabobian guilt.[2]

---

2. *[Telephone Pole 345] Telephone cable in cracked yellow tube.*

BC Collateral

JOSEPH FERONE

The bus stopped
before the pawnshop window:
I went to the guitars,
you went to the knives.

Meals on Wheels,
nineteen eighty-eight

MARIA SAMMARCO

The Inner City in a long delivery list today, in and out the downtown hotels.
　　Driving left on Powell,
stop at the Hotel Europe's pointed corner, brass and cut glass by Angelo Calori,
a lesson in an art to be learned. Loop around Carrall and Hastings,
down to Columbia Hotel. Red flag on the delivery card: AIDS. First encounter.
　　I slowly cross the room, but he is gentle, his fear of rejection,
and for his young girl in the Okanagan he may not be allowed to see again,
as bad as his condition.
　　At Cordova and Abbott, the ghost of Harkley and Haywood salutes me,
the oldest sporting goods store after sixty-three years, gone, in foreclosure.
　　At Winters Hotel in the middle of the block, through the red door,
up steps to the red balcony, open at each floor to the red stairwell.
No one around, except a woman in an emerald silk shirt, welcoming me
at the reception counter, a silent smile on vermilion lips.
　　At Hotel Balmoral, Hastings and Main, I open the pub door by mistake.
The heavy hot humid stench of beer at lunch time cuts off my breath.
Eyed by drunken men, I panic — but by the Styrofoam box I carry,
I am safe — up steps of stained carpet, along the narrow hallway,
at the dim light I check numbers, a new face, a glimpse into a secluded life.
　　Next address. Hastings and Main. Carnegie Hall. A crowd, crowding
out the sunshine. The vapour of public toilets suddenly takes me back
to Djemaâ el Fna square, Marrakech, with carriages, horses, mobile layers
of human life. The Sun Building towers over the hollows of these low hotels,
the pulsating sickness of the city hidden in a brick skin.

Jackson avenue and *east* hastings

BUD OSBORN

little bird barely feathered
fallen from your nest prematurely
flexing wings too weak to lift you
from this hard luck street corner
of heavy traffic and hungry predators
how long will you survive little bird?
will the miracle within your tiny wings
save you in time?

or the little girl barely dressed
across the street on her own dangerous corner
waving thin and frail arms
attracting like your wings
not flight but the attention
of killers?

pender street east

JIM WONG-CHU

fresh rock cod
a pleasant smile
roast pork fresh hot
taste before you buy
(guarantee to satisfy)
ginger green onions
soy sauce   msg

take a break
across the street
find a booth
order green tea
relax…
where else would you possibly
want to be?

curtain of rain

JIM WONG-CHU
from Paul Yee

curtain of rain
another act unfolds

chinatown
forever changing
you and I
actors audience
watching being watched

pender street east
nothing dampens its spirit

quiet yet dignified
unassuming yet proud
hidden under umbrellas
steady as raindrops

Grandmothers in Chinatown

JANCIS M. ANDREWS

They seem boneless, these women, twigs of black
pants and dragon-embroidered jacket, shuffling
between family and franchise
on a culture still alien
after fifty years.
Their jet eyes reveal nothing
except an onyx patience: apology —
or intuition, maybe — for living.
Stung by my Wasp eye, they twitch
their gaze to oriental jungles
of shark fins, birds' nests, clasping
grandchildren: small sprigs of cherry blossom
by the hand.
What do they have to teach me,
the loudmouthed, white-skinned giantess
from British Properties, crashing the barrier
of Chinatown's East Pender Street and Main?
What do I know of dragons, however silken,
that stalk their sleep?
How do you enter a language
shaped like twigs
even though those twigs
be cherry blossom?

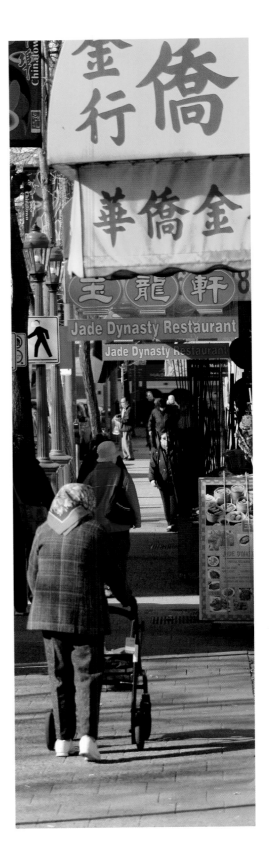

Sun Yat-Sen's garden

PAM GALLOWAY

1.
Once, you showed me the prairies
where the sky teaches meditation, absorbs
unspoken wishes and, on cold clear nights,
fires them back on iridescent stems.

Here, where rain draws down sky close
to earth, I proffer gardens; this one
inside white walls, its classical sculptures,
water and stones,
subliminal drone,

a great blue heron waits, perfectly posed
beside bamboo and laurels.
Is it real? You watch for an eye
to blink you into belief.

2.
Coming from iced-white winter, you show me
the strangeness of open store-fronts
in January, shop-keepers in thin coats and no hats.

I show you fat frogs in Chinatown that swell and burp
and flap their feet in a shallow bath,
eels unable to stop swimming, going nowhere,
writing s over and over.

After you leave, I return to buy a frog,
the biggest and loudest, take it
to Sun Yat-Sen's garden, set it down
beside the pond, watch it leap
into the green-shadowed dark.

moonshine

DAPHNE MARLATT
for Carole

start   for the tracks   let's go let's start   february morning dark not dark
at all but full   end of the alley end of a night full moon rides   telephone
poles barring the sky moon's face ashine & all our houses dark

let's go, he says, eager to start for the tracks for the train for that idea south
moon stays *allons!* night-alley & i halfpulled from sleep to wipe inside
the windshield   lunar light makes moist   lunacy begetting look!
clearing the glass to stare   all dewy one   dew-dropping, down-
turning through wires & poles that scaffold west & buzz still
spawning old woes (old) stories shed   spilled   scattered
abroad

                                        the way they came   building where water was
on the edge of the tracks a litter of shacks little of what remained a bright
idea: *go west*   they came fell under the moon drawn out to streets where they
could trade on rhythm & wit   high for days

                                        & east of us the roofline sharpens now

let's start, he cries, my eager child   in the dark of the year   moon shines
one ray of, on a sleeping woman   *musaeos* her son, moon man or moon-
inspired   his storehouse of stories bright in the dark   it's grandmother's
eye inside   who broods   brooms   beams down passageways

the future a kind of light on the other side   not morning yet   on the rim
they got off the train & just walked in 'like i'd been here all my life'
'at six or seven in the morning you'd hear the music going' in the cabins
moon-inspired at the dice game   moon or wine

it was craps   it was scraps   of song in the turn of a phrase scattered
along old walkways edge of the Creek   crap   comes up with the dew

this lowlying ground between two waters *west of the moon*

a series of small hills big talk wood smoke neighbourly cask uncorked
in the crack between two dawns   cop knock

                                        not dark tonight, but full
of moonshine muse-meant memory-talk down laneways 'wide enough for
horsedrawn carts' '& the horse ran away'   with all their stories *alée*
gallery for walking we drive along (their faces sleeping) so we know
where we are in light of their passing

on these alley stories
yours, moon, going & gone.

Sam's Shirt Shop on Hastings

BARBARA PELMAN

On Saturdays, I helped my father in his store —
my parents' idea of bonding and cheap labour —
and I, a reluctant nine-year-old,
straightened the sweaters and ties
at Sam's Shirt Shop on Hastings and Abbott.
You could win a free pair of socks if you could say
"Sam's Shirt Shop" five times without stumbling.
Nobody could. My father waited patiently
for customers, a game of solitaire laid out
for the long hours in between.
I liked lunch best — a chance to wander,
to peek into Woodward's holiday windows
where mechanical elves worked and whistled
and toy trains chugged the perimeters
of the miniature North Pole.
At the Oyster Bar and Grill I bought
sliced egg sandwiches on white buns
and milkshakes. We sat in the back of the store
and sometimes my father sang, but mostly
we were quiet, trying hard to learn each other.

Alleyway, 8 a.m.

CATHERINE OWEN
for Goh Poh Seng

The last rooster on Victoria Drive
crows from a dark shed.

In the wake of the garbage truck,
rats and starlings survive. This then

is what you've always called freedom.
A man sipping coffee in a stark garden shouts

at me — *What address are you wanting?*
Asphalt opens its mouth to utter.

Fennel. Bindweed. Forget-me-nots.
The skyline's wounding sharpens.

Raspberries ripen outside of fences.
Their wilderness and my tongue.

Engulfed is not a word
we save for love.

Evening on Victoria

GOH POH SENG
for Margaret Joyce

The evening breeze
plucks at the trees
like a master pipa player
the strings of his instrument,
itself surely fashioned
by man's intuitive genius,
the miracle of his inherent talents.

As they danced
the leaves whispered
love's tender verses
like we used to do decades ago
when our own hearts and souls
sought to fuse together
though certainly not as ardent as today.

The nearby mountains lean nearer
casting shadows at my feet
while the far firmament
approaches us in the twilight
driving flocks of black birds home
feathers incandescent
in the final light,
replete from their day-long hunting
down by the shore.

My day now also nearly spent
there is an urgent need to return
home to you, my beloved wife
who waits, always,
as I complete my day's day-dreaming.

The man who lives in the gazebo

CHRIS HUTCHINSON

The man who lives in the gazebo in the park in this
ineloquent metropolis — we've dreamt he has nothing
but what the rain gives him in his sleep: riches
of a presence, fingers tapping, silver-ringed,
what a child hears of voices, pure plash
of a cadence loosed from sense. This morning
work-bound strangers, mutely trampling
the many-eyed, the dew-decked blades of grass
step around him, living shadows, unrepentant
in their trespass. While across the bay the city
clears its throat but never speaks — as language
is held within us as we sleep: words,
whose meanings fold in on themselves,
on waking, shut the door.

SeaBus

GEORGE WHIPPLE

One of those
blue blowzy days,
sunglint rocketing
off rocks as our
SeaBus backs
out into the bay.
Hackles of
white chop.
Sprees of spray.
Guliwings furling
and unfurling
in our wake…
til North Vancouver
comes in view:

20 storey high
steel pterodactyl
cranes as delicate
as dragonflies
hovering onshore
as swift snowfields
ski toward us as we dock
— one lone loon bobbing
in our aftershock,
one happy flag
having an orgasm
with the wind, and
not one cloud
in the sky.

When the big hand is on the starfish

RUSSELL THORNTON

When the big hand is on the starfish
and the little hand is on the crab, you're looking up
at the lobby clock. It's six o'clock. Now a flock
of Canada Geese, tinted sea-green, rays of the sun
blazing over them, flies past a mass of sea life —
lobsters, turtles, sea snails, skate, make their way
through forests of seaweed. This is outside,
within the arched entranceway. Seahorses, pufferfish,
traced in terracotta, swim the front wall face
as along inlet shore rock. The same biplane
flies by twice, three times, then the same Zeppelin —
here, it is, after all, 1930, and has been since 1930,
when this was the tallest edifice in the entire
British Commonwealth. When the big hand
is on the starfish and the little hand
is on the lobster, it's three o'clock. Boats and ships
go by — the Resolution, the Golden Hind,
the HMS Egeria, the Sonora, the Empress of Japan.
Inside again, at the five brass elevator doors,
above which sailing vessels burst out of waves
with lighting in their prows, stand five female
elevator operators, chosen for their beauty,
wearing sailor uniforms, female usherers
into hardwood interiors like those of ships' cabins —
1930 is also 2009, and now they're the flowing light
that chooses the lobby's stained glass windows
for their beauty, and the zodiac pictured
on the polished marble floor. When the big hand
is on the starfish and the little hand
is on the turtle, it's two o'clock. Terracotta
Canada Geese fly along the buiding's sides
to meet above the brass-framed main glass doors.
This is the Marine Building, address, number 355
on a street named for Sir Harry Burrard, ex-shipmate
and friend of the ship's captain who, at the behest
of His Majesty's Royal Navy, sailed the water-globe
in search of a mysterious sea-route, failed,
yet discovered and mapped the waters of this place.
When the big hand is on the starfish
and the little hand is on the sea snail, it's nine o'clock,
and I'm nine or is it seven years old, turning
the page in Haig-Brown's *Captain of the Discovery*
where the captain and a dozen of his crew
sail in the ship's yawl through the tree-branch-
overhung narrows into the inlet. Now people
from the nation whose home is the north shore
put off in canoes to greet them and offer
freshly cooked smelts. The Englishman at once
orders his men to shorten sail and allow
the canoes to keep pace. Now he looks out
across the inlet — which he will name for Sir Harry B.
The geese that fly across his sails, and past
the bright brass buttons on George Vancouver's
blue naval coat, fly now through the brass rays
of the sun rising on the Marine Building
entranceway's dazzling horizon, framing
the Discovery. When the big hand
is on the starfish and the little hand is on the crab,
it's six o'clock again. For an instant
or is it a lifetime, terracotta geese pass
into living geese — and back again, Art Deco.
They pass through where illustrious ships
sail by and famous buildings stand. They pass
through to living geese like the seahorses pass
through to drifting seahorses, like the starfishes
to crawling starfishes, purple arms, tube feet
that latch on to surfaces, slowly decorating time.

Cathedral

MEREDITH QUARTERMAIN

Holy Rosary gothic revival
Salvation Army stone, brick
Suzette's sandwiches
Cathedral Square
where coal-baron Dunsmuir
crosses carpet-bagger Richards —
men, boys, in cheap track-pants
slouch on benches under an arch
of scaffolding —
squeegee kid leans on its concrete pillar —
the night's street-light steely grey
face of a backpacker on the church steps.

Soup to salvation, General Booth said,
my soldiers are saved to save —
build shelters, hostels, farms, nurseries,
hospitals, half-way houses, language classes.
Volunteer work's what holds society together
(the premier in his government address
to the Army) — $2.7 billion worth a year.
In Victoria, we're going door-to-door
for $45,000. We've got 326 shelter beds.
And we're helping people with disabilities
find rewarding employment.

In the square the men trade hits or cigarettes
under a vaulting of stars.

Whore in the eddy

HEATHER HALEY

Gazes up at ballooning clouds as if imagining
frogs. Giraffes. Corvettes and barns.
As if Neptune's head has heard
her pleas. Sent me. She looks like a mannequin.
As if by law of nature, a stripped woman's body
looks like a mannequin after it floats
to the surface in a rainforest denuded
by steam donkeys and timber sales. All matter
from the depths is netted by log jams.

She stares at me. Cannot see
the pebbles embedded in my knees.
Or my face, not so sweet.
No bubbles, just the stillness
of standing water. No trace DNA.
No hard-earned cash. Only cool airstreams
of aspen leaves. My grasping hand
takes hers, skin gliding onto my fingers
like a glove. A device. We share features
any porno-masticating, regular working stiff
joe wants in his garage
between the red pickup and the Crestliner.

We watch the rim of night, a coiled arm
of stars, their slow light two million
years too late. Naked eyes decipher
Orion the hunter. Cassiopeia. Bright knots
of the Double Cluster. Mars appears.
I look the other way, to the North Star.

Words on the streets

BERNICE LEVER

First, here's the 2 H's: Homely Homer and Hamming Hamilton,
sandwiching Gorgeous Georgia and Randy throbbing Robson
which just happen to caress Vancouver's Library Square
that's definitely not square, just Roman ruins or rounds
and CBC Plaza, not level, but certainly, 3-D tented studios.
That old Greek poet would've loved this repeat of Babel:
chanting, crooning, ranting on his namesake thoroughfare
which is not faring too well on this September Sunday
as these ego-mad orators have mobs of looky lou's grabbing
literary handouts, and packs of children racing for the freebies,
as autograph hounds are baying at frazzled, finger-cramped writers
pretending to listen or even hear amid the hubbub swirling
about their ears (literacy lost) at so called, "Word on the Street"
which really is a raucous medley of city traffic and
"buy my book" pleas as wanne-be writers failing to snag
any agents, editors and publishers pause before Randy Robson's
ample stone band stand for a few hip hopping notes, thus
uplifted, they whirl by children's tables and clowning giants
ever hopeful of a nano-second of fame at CBC's beckoning
mics, "Tell us your name" in crowded skin-burnt sunshine or
in rain-soaked tiers, at hoity-toity Hamilton's hamming central.
Next desperate for shelter, they end this crammed, noisy circuit
to Glamorous Georgia and her poetry bus, yes, finally,
accepting to be near a poet in a confined space, yet
watching the literary/literacy hungry hordes swarming by,
avid newcomers always yearning for more word projectiles,
on Homer, Hamilton, Robson and Georgia.

Under Christchurch bells

AISLINN HUNTER

It's eight p.m. and over the city the bells of Christchurch
Cathedral start ringing.

   But something is wrong.
The clang and brawn of the bells fall out of tune and order,
without remorse, like an argument between the bell ringer and God,

the clamour pealing out from the tower, and all of us
on the street and in our houses look over: see a dark steeple,
the quick glint of its bells.

Tolling, they sound out over False Creek, climb the hill
towards Kitsilano, the noise like a bull run through town,
stopping only at dead ends and doorways,
the ground reverberating, and panes of glass in the barber shop,
the mini-mart windows warble with each hard note.

There are countries where towns are still built around their churches.
Houses and shops fanning out like a crinoline skirt from the body,
towns where bells ring out over everyone and everything
in even benediction —

The woman in her window looks towards the cathedral
and the buses on Pender idle alongside the road;
the chestnut trees have filled with birds, suddenly afraid to fly.

In the bell tower hands pull hard on ropes
that are capable of music,
   but perhaps this too is a song,
the hands belonging to a man who is finding his place
in the middle of this city,
who finds a chorus of open mouths with him,
ringing out against the hour.

What Jack Shadbolt said

TREVOR CAROLAN

Here's how he said *adios*
the last time we spoke,
by the entrance to the VAG, not long
before the end,
skin thin as rice-paper:

"Art is experience given form.
I follow things expressively that interest me;
and try to express the experience of change that has
happened to me.
My feeling now is that art is a matter of finding coherence,
unity; that deep down everyone wants to be an artist;
if my experience is valid
it might be valid for somebody else…

It's good to see you, boys."

Happy Hour: Bacchus Lounge

LYNDA GRACE PHILIPPSEN

The pianist lurches through
Autumn Leaves without feeling
and the din of chit-chat pushes at the ceiling.

No matter its shape, a piano
out of tune is anything but grand.
The Armani suit one table over brags

he's not been sober since Tuesday last;
the pair of stilettos with him,
malpractice lawyer, blows her nose

into her napkin and lays it on the table.
That settles it. I leave behind
more than I drank. Across the room

a waiter lifts a glass, polishes the rim
and sets it back on a table for two.
The pianist hashes *The Very Thought of You*.

How you would mock my desire.
How you would hate it here —
maroon velvet, black marble, cold fire.

Scaffolding

MEREDITH OUARTERMAIN

Plato's Necessity holds a rainbow pillar buttressing the heavens. A great whorl within which seven other whorls slowly spin the other way, each one carrying a singing Siren and the Fates: Clotho, Lachesis, and Atropos. The spinner, the giver of lots, the shears on the thread of life — these are the daughters of Necessity.

Here in human scaffolding, the courthouse: an imaginary arena. From Roman senators weighing a case of treason, in the torchlight of the Curia. Or the centumviri judging thieves and frauds in Basilica Julia — its vaulted ceilings and clerestory windows 100 feet above palatial chambers. In the courtrooms of modernism, the law is low, flat, rectilinear, with model trees.

The courthouse steps — they settled on the Courthouse steps, built a cabin — fan out in concrete slabs up a pyramid anthill of registries and chambers, ending mid-sentence at a wall, water rushing over it — no Roman columns — just a 10-foot wall of justness — pediments and scroll-top columns gone to the art-gallery — a glass roof, an arcade, an atrium over its low flat concrete. Glass on metal scaffold over the hush of carpeting, potted plants, blind-folded Themis, French *escafe*, a shell, Latin *scapha*, a light boat, a skiff; Greek *skaphe*, a trough. Anne Boleyn on the scaffold took the fatal stroke.

Outside the courthouse, a woman with a crutch scoops water for her windshield squeegee with globalized burger-joint paper cups. A teen in low-slung jeans coolly tilts her buttock as she drifts up Howe Street. Live to Love, says the Celine / Dior trapeze-woman swinging out from a billboard.

Inside the courts, the buzzing of innumerable bees: If your Ladyship, Lordship would turn to page nine-hundred and fifty of the transcript. My friend and I have reached an agreement, subject to your Ladyship, Lordship's approval. I'm afraid I must ask your Ladyship, Lordship for an adjournment to review the sixteen binders of new evidence. Objection, M'Lady, M'Lord, my friend has asked a leading question. A moment please, M'Lady, M'Lord. If it would please M'Lady, M'Lord to refer to exhibit A. I believe, M'Lady, M'Lord, it's under tab 100W of binder I2C. Those are all my questions. M'Lady, M'Lord.

Listening in

CHRISTOPHER LEVENSON

During the war posters told us
"Careless talk costs lives!"
so we kept our lips zippered.
In a bus on Burrard Street
a man just released from St. Paul's
answers his cell phone,
gives details to a friend of how
his underarm cyst was drained.
All privacy long since dead,
complicit, we spy upon
our fellow passengers.

Erasure at Westcoast Tattoo

ANDREA DANCER

Storefront man in his muscle
shirt, a devil in design,
shows her the eraser and a needle
eight inches long.

She offers up her nose as
rat dog tiptoes past, the hoop
in his one dog-ear jangling
confession.

Between here and there,
demons and dragons writhe,
women and tigers pounce,
the phoenix stares over

one shoulder; these walls
jumpin' like a juice joint.

Her head backs up, her nostril twists, his inked
thumb jams the eraser, pink
rubber waiting steel, the hot
tip hammered through and out.

Outside, the street drills
the concrete past into
noone nowhere where
the building never ends.

She's travelling
far now behind
the cement behind her eyes,
riding light right
through the piercing,
the promise.

Where the numbers meet the trees

LESLIE TIMMINS

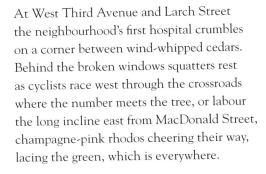

At West Third Avenue and Larch Street
the neighbourhood's first hospital crumbles
on a corner between wind-whipped cedars.
Behind the broken windows squatters rest
as cyclists race west through the crossroads
where the number meets the tree, or labour
the long incline east from MacDonald Street,
champagne-pink rhodos cheering their way,
lacing the green, which is everywhere.

Dogwood, fir, spruce — a forest interstice among house lots,
where eagles, impossibly large, impossibly wide, skim north,
and herons, pterodactyl-winged, float south across
some undivided divide.
To the west, street names bear the burden of wars.
At Burrard Bridge sunlight chills in the absence
of Senakw. But here, and nearest,
this is where we wed,
where our cat lost an eye and lived,
where thousands, every summer, fill the sidewalks
to see fireworks and return home in the dark in peace.
Daily the flight path of herons lifts us,
the justice of trees breathes for all — yew, larch, balsam, pine
quelling the pattern, opening the house of the mind.

---

*Senakw, or Snauq, was a village of the Coast Salish peoples (now known as First Nations)
before government made the land into a reserve, and later forced the people to relocate.

The crosstown bus

JOHN PASS

I'd forgotten how dark the city
from the empty fluorescent bus

and how warm the dark upon
stepping down. As a young man

I'd walk with a young man's arrogance
sure you'd be at the party, picking up

your scent and song already on the expectant
air. You'd be there ahead of me a little

on Pine Street, leading me on, the music
behind us, before I knew your name.

On my broken leg

Vancouver General

LIONEL KEARNS

General or local? asked
the anaesthetist. I glanced
at the instruments: scalpels
scissors, suture-stapler,
a wrench for the lug-bolts
and a shiny electric drill,
the same kind I use at home.
I muttered ... *general.*

Fire alarm

GEORGE STANLEY

At 5:30 this morning when the fire alarm went off
all of us apartment-dwellers, strangers, gathered
out on the sidewalk to escape the noise —

The cool Sunday morning that had not yet been turned
into yuppie brunch — it had a hundred
directions to look —

It was the cool air, the sun behind clouds —
the street lights snapped off — it was all of us
strangers & no structure.

Purgatory

CHRISTINE SCHRUM

The man with tight black curls
and leather coffins for shoes
presses a card into your palm,
tells you to call sometime —
you're new to this burg,
need someone to show you around.
You're at Wicked Café, fittingly
situated on Hemlock at 7th
beside the Lotus Eaters
restaurant. The walls have chains
and the heady reggae and hot
frothy mocha are narcoleptics,
leaving you warm and emboldened
so you say yes, you'll call,
and the man rubs his oily hands
and smiles. A stooped woman walks in,
wheeling a sleeping seraph
in a squeaky stroller. The child's face is haloed
with sticky curls and toast crumbs
and it reminds you, for some reason,
of wide-open, golden Iowa
and the friends you left behind.
The psychiatrist to your left
is telling her friend about the ideal
antidepressant cocktail, how the world
is black and white newsprint without it.
You lick the cream off an angelic cloud
of carrot cake, silently praying
the tattooed Aussie Gods
who run this place will someday
know your name.

99 Express — 8 a.m.

BIBIANA TOMASIC

I am lush on the bus
in a green and fuzzy coat, reading,
when a male in a red jacket hesitates,
then sits down beside me.
I am still reading
when I notice his thick fingers
resting on his thigh
and spot his long blonde curls
and his brown beard
in the speck of my eye,
imagine those curls hovering
rocking over me
when he drops his hand between
his legs and I wish I could see
more. He seems like an outdoor type,
a climber or camper,
but he doesn't smell like one,
which is good,
and I am still reading when he crosses
his left leg over his right
in a fluid motion
and his foot, wearing sensible shoes,
bends back by the seat in front.
I am still reading when I know
he must be a climber, by the angle
of his ankle, sustained this way
for a long time and I know
he must be very flexible
and I consider this implication
on both a physical and psychological
level. Angles are good in bed.
I am still reading
when he squirms, looks at me once,
then again; so I scan
my furry mantle, realize
I have turned into a large pulsing
vagina, right there
on the acrylic seat of the B-Line,
but I keep reading
don't notice him licking his mouth
as he descends the back exit stairs,
turns off Broadway and walks south on Granville.

The fourth moon of Broadway

RON SMITH

This is the avenue I remember, straight and wide.
This is the city of trees at night, fired
from the belly-busting rage and swagger that chain
brother to brother. This is the city that dwells
in the tribal power of invincible youth, the will
to walk the streets in the glow of making history
from hunger and blood, the blood of prisoner and lover alike.
I wait for those who watch the slanting rain
and seek the flesh of new bone, flowers bursting into the sky
out of the appetite of skeletons, the orange blooms of night
shucked from the fourth moon of Broadway, melons
glowing overhead in the nightmare chambers
of storefronts. This is not Damascus, though dusk burns
everlasting in the recitation of the names of our beloved.
This is the will of the deal; to host the flesh reborn
from solitude, to linger at the height of orgasm.
This is the gift I hold in moonlight, soft
and transparent, open to what the heart and body crave.
This is the avenue I remember, straight and wide.

Quinte*
(Goddess on Tenth Avenue)

KAROLY SANDOR

Are you in my house to advise me
which vegetables to buy,
music to choose, to comment on the paintings,
adjust the thermostat and convince me of my right
to dance in the sunshine naked under the cherry tree?

Are you in the city to re-draft its beaches,
to count its pebbles and comb its trees,
to assign new parabolas for the landing of loons
and prescribe the number of lovers
per square kilometre?

Are you on this continent
to measure its contraction,
to oversee the changing of seasons,
control its tides,
the direction and velocity of winds?

Are you on this planet to supervise its orbit,
design its sky's damask,
stir the colours for its rainbows,
compose its earthquakes,
conduct its volcanoes? — What do you mean — Yes?!

Then what are you doing in my bed?
If your father finds out he will kill you!
What I do think of the origin of the Universe
or whether I am of star-stuff I cannot tell,
my mouth is full of your hair.

*The fifth recognized parrying position to protect the head (in sabre fencing)
and to protect the lower inside of the body in foil and epée fencing.

Point Grey, Saturday paper

MARK COCHRANE

At the corner of 4th & Alma
the busker with grey, rock-star locks
drops his banjo case & trades
quips with a barrister
I happen to know, dapper outside Muffin Break
in his Gore-Tex & fleece —

Now this is news. Such a pair
bent at the hips & grinning
with January breath
at four mugshots of our premier, intoxicate
on the front page of the *Globe*, its
coin box beneath the stoplights.

I remember that busker. With case yawning
he clowns for children's change
outside the liquor store
in the underground parkade: Puff
the Magic Dragon. And one night
last April, the wrong consort & I, intoxicate,
stumbled into him
near Bimini's
past closing. He was loaded
with wisdom, warned us
not to have kids, then
from double-take & eye parley
sleuthed our scenario: he peered
straight into the glass box
of my face & said,
The missteps of a single night, my friend — you pay
for these, one loonie at a time,
a lifetime.

Then, laughing: Or you *don't*.

Quayside

EVELYN LAU

After hearing the news
of your cancer, for days I felt hungry.
The tulips hung their heads in the hot room.
Sunlight pressed my forehead
like a feverish hand, and the white bed
came unmoored, a raft on a sea of nightmares.
Then I walked down to the marina, and through
the transparent water saw a sea star,
purple as wine, splashed on a rock,
a crab showing me its soft belly,
the bouquet of stones in blues and greys
as rare as orchids — and then I saw that for years
you have existed all around me
like they say heaven already does,
your voice which hour after hour slipped over my skin
like silk, so that even now when I close my eyes
I am clothed in it, there, in the green office
where we had for years and years
our one conversation. I was always waiting
for you, and when you arrived shivering
and smiling in the glass doorway,
wearing your woven coat, of which you said
there was only one in the whole world,
together we climbed the cigarette-stained stairs
to the room we built with words.
Here a Granny Smith apple bobs in the saltwater,
skin green as paint, and a seagull stabs it with its beak
while another circles nearby, weeping
with want, and when I look again the apple
is in the mouth of a crow carrying to a rooftop,
and then beyond, into the sky.
The bed of crushed mussel shells, bruise-black,
the silent glide of the scarlet freighter,
the wind slapping my face awake
to the world somersaulting blue and brazen —
I am gulping the air flavoured with metal and shellfish,
stretching to take it in, salt sting, sea grass,
gold pollen detonating in the breeze, the profusion
of it, this life you returned to me, this one life.

The Sylvia

GEORGE FETHERLING

Vines grow thick and knotted
that squirrels might use them
as a staircase to peek into the
rooms of lovers peering out.
They hope for a little food
or failing that a safe glimpse
of how life is pursued
on the other side of the glass.

People told me, I that lacked amber,
to warn of change or promise it:
a traffic signal with only green and red
with no light to separate joy from impatience.
They were avid for such metaphors
as this.

Now I have real amber mounted
in a silver ring and live at the Sylvia Hotel
where the only way to know the season
is to look out the window and note the
colour of the ivy.

Half the year, the green of
first life. Otherwise the waxy red
of the reborn emotion we hope exists
in case we ever need it.

Seawall Stanley Park

JULIA VAN GORDER

Here
we come together   where
the salt air meets
the warm-berried air of the land,
and rainbow spinnakers burst
in salute to the fitful sun.

I am with you, jogger,
in your paddy green shorts.
You, woman, carefully dress'd
and dog'd.
You, lovemaking couple,
oblivious to us.
You, lone man on a bench,
your back to us.

Here
we come together and   a part

The poet with stones has moved

JULIA VAN GORDER

The poet with stones has moved
his stone clan nearer Second Beach.
The sea will still destroy it there, Poet,
but I want to tell you I saw it
in all its beauty — the birds and animals
and abstracts joining, enhancing the humans.
Or are they humans?
What is a human? That young woman,
scantily clad, running for her life?
That couple of men engaging each other?
That aged woman walking her Yorkie?
We too, in all our beauty,
will be knocked down, destroyed,
replaced by other clans, in all their beauty.

December aquarium

SHANNON STEWART

In the Vancouver aquarium
electric eels are rigged
to light up a Christmas tree.
Bulbs flicker on and off
as the eels slide in their tank,
grey and divorced from the miracle
they work. Battle-scarred,
they swim in tired circles,
eyes shards of milk glass,
clouded from too many electric jolts.

We move through the corridors
as if we were still lovers,
not wanting to ask why we came
to this gloom, why look in on a world
blooming so wildly under the glass.
You stop by an empty aquarium,
press your hands to the window,
blood etched only in the creases
of your palms. An octopus shoots
from its cave to climb the blue light,
a sac of puckered skin
taking the deliberate breaths
of an ancient engine.
It chugs backwards,
ragged arms undulating
like bed sheets shaken
in the air, scattering
hair and dreams to the wind.
The suction cups glued
between us, hundreds
of tightening kisses.

Below this theatre of flesh,
is the ocean floor, luminous,
with bruises of starfish,
purple and blood orange,
five fingers hard about the rocks.
Here, the most desperate clutches
are given room, the hidden mouth
drinks from stone.

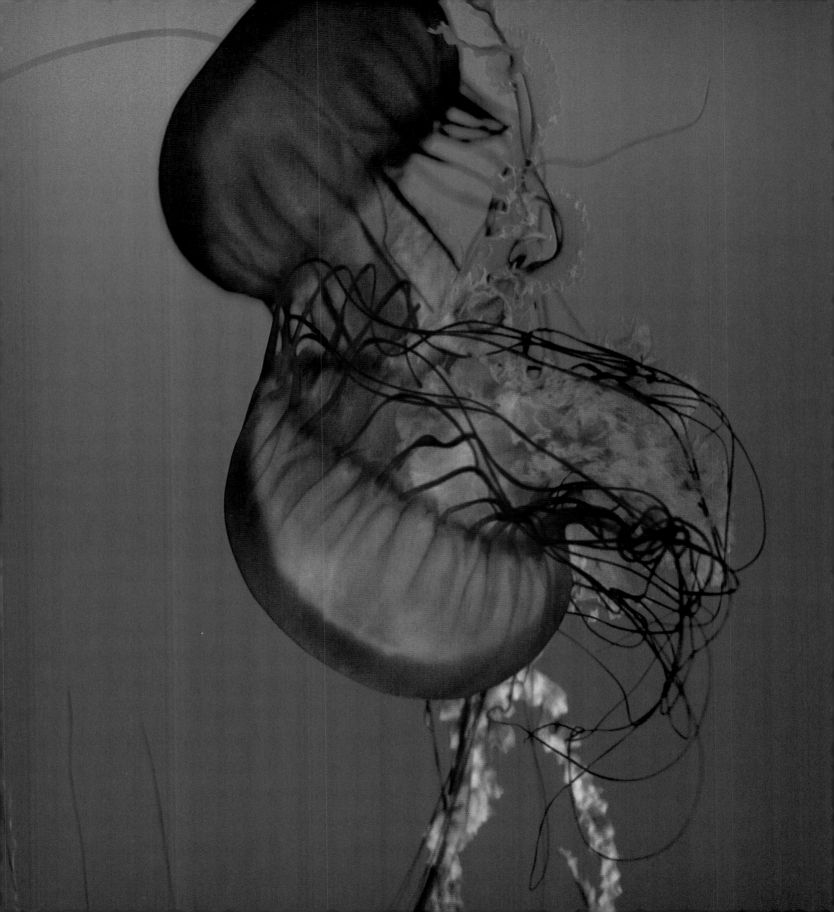

Heronry

MAUREEN HYNES

The true name for this heronry
is cacophony. As we cross the parking lot,
approach the dozen trees that hold
aloft twenty-six heron nests,
the chicks' *tuk-tuk-tuk* intensifies madly.
The leaves beneath the nests are streaked
white with guano, the cars spotted and striped.
Fifty chicks, two to a nest, are arguing again,
spilling and pushing, and flapping their newly enormous wings.
They are learning how to hold each others'
beaks still for future courting and fighting. Is this
henhouse or ceremony, we wonder, the schoolyard
at recess or the lesson itself?

No wonder the heron escapes
to gaze motionless at the water's edge,
craving solitude so much she stands on one leg,
her silent mirrored double her only company.

On the death of the Lions Gate Bridge

ELIZABETH BACHINSKY

You can see her from the sea. You can see cars
inch north and south under the gift of lights
a beer man gave to Vancouver's sky at night.
Strung tighter than a piano, she's tuned to both
shores — nightmarish, the *idea* you can't get across,
slight, anachronistic, from a distance
thin as a hair crawling with pestilent traffic.
But, in the evening, cool air curls in through the narrows
and the traffic calms,
and lovers sit in one another's arms
at Prospect Point and behold her. How we love
to look at what we keep and what we have.
When she comes down at last, the future comes.
With it, other lovers. Other charms.

Silver thaw

DIANE SUTHERLAND

When my mother and her friends were young
winter was colder
snow fell in deep swells
and the lagoon
always froze over,
ducks and swans folded into smooth feather-stones atop the ice
while the geese still flew south.

In the cold quiet of such a winter night,
my mother and her friends,
filled with the heat of youthful mischief,
laughing in the icy eve as though it were a spring day,
rolled and rolled and pushed and pushed huge snow-balls
onto the road, blocking the causeway through the tall trees,
the only way to get to the only bridge
that crossed the sea inlet to the northern shore.

The night sizzled with their energy
and the snow began to melt as they slipped and slid,
impelling their glorious creation into position.
But when they finished their chore the chill air returned,
the barricade frozen into a solid mass, a silver thaw.

With morning came the road workers,
burning up the hours,
to set loose the road from its icy shackle.
Years later my mother still laughed,
her beautiful voice rising in the warmth.

Fish candy

ALLAN SAFARIK

Stripped cod skeletons
twisted heads and tails
glassy eyes stare at soft dreams
Not a cloud in the blue sky
A barrel of undressed fish
show translucent bones
in the soft Pacific light
A man in a crumpled overcoat
wine stains and a toothless grin
stops by and digs his penknife
into the heads dislodging eyeballs
tosses them into the air
catches each one in his mouth
with a loud sucking sound

A herring gull on the rooftop
swooping down misses the air born
eyeball and pecks the man hard
in the middle of his face
leaving a brighter red spot than
on the forehead of an east indian wife
Later he's trying to explain
how it happened to some dock workers
But the sun was too hot and big
drops of blood fell silently
from the hole in his head
When the cops asked who hit him
he muttered about a feed of fish candy
and being mugged by a big bird

When he left in the police car
the bird on the roof was laughing
at him while he banged on the window
On the ride up to Main Street
he was warned not to bleed on the seats
Nurse said stitches wouldn't improve him
More like a beer bottle than a bird
the judge said sentencing him
to ten days for being drunk
and disorderly in a public place
but gave him credit for the story
Fish candy and a big bird is all
he said when he went to jail
They understood completely

Babies' Cottage

JOHN DONLAN

Where do we come from?
What are we?
Where are we going?
Don't ask.

The mountains across the harbour
were a chain of offshore islands
before their long slow crash
into British Columbia.

The ground we walk on, hard-packed clay and gravel,
was carried down the mountains
by glaciers and rivers now vanished.
The hospice around the corner

once housed family court;
before that it was Babies' Cottage, an orphanage.
Someone sits by a lamp in the fog-shrouded lounge.
Above the fog, we are told, the sun is shining.

The crabs under the Second Narrows Bridge

BRIAN BRETT

The scaffolding of the bridge
collapsed like a tinkertoy,
a folding accordion of men
hurled into shadows against the sun,
flightless birds that were
a gift from the garish sky.

The scavenger crabs,
eyes on stalks
found a new feast
in the cobwebs of the greasy brain,
living on memories of hammers
and lawns that needed mowing.

Then they spit out
little bubbles of blood,
a rising stream
that marked every man's grave.

Now the men inhabit the crabs,
the trace of each face
delicately etched
on the barnacle-crusted shells,
wide eyes looking for the sky.

At night, the orange-red husks
clatter their claws; it's a
secret conversation in code
revealing the real mechanics
behind the construction of crabs.

You can hear them
tapping out their dreams

as the clicking ghosts
build under water
a whispering bridge of claws.

Museum

OANA AVASILICHIOAEI

when
a column
of smoke
is a column
steam   is   confused

when when is an artefact
when is

if a boy   a figure
if a park   dreams
                  we receive a dowry
                  green

a merry-go-round
          built   1912
                  we read quickly, confident

                  though   misled
          1917   says another

if a puzzle
          wasn't so utterly trustworthy

then we were   vacuous
we let language wander as if she could have her pick of many suitors

          mindful   I stay calm
          mindful   of those 36
                  wooden horses carved by prisoners' hands
          I stay

when was it built exactly?

1904   says a third

if a merry-go-round could   remember

I am twirling   restored, removed, canopied,
pink-cherubed, mirrored, filigreed   I am twirling
though at the centre
                  still

The crows cope

DIANE TUCKER

Under bridges, brushing the undersides of charcoal clouds, clasping
the sides of blue garbage bins, scratching and scolding, they pick
diamonds out of our refuse, shine obsidian in what passes for sunlight,
tip their conical heads to make pearly light on their beaks,
pin our hopes to their black breasts as they rush eastward by the hundreds,
rush at sunset, soar to Still Creek to recycle everything that we refuse,
that they can turn to sterling, cackles and throat scratches, black shoulders,

wingtips' airless flakes of light in the scrub woods between the railroad tracks,
in needle-pocked city parks, in the rose bush in the back yard, on the tarpaper roof.

The crows know our places as we know our own fingers, have assumed
their turf as we raised and flailed it in their faces. Just holding tight
has gotten them the sky, the waterblue skinny monkey-bar clouds,
the wet-fiery west and the grey days, wet and heavy, sheets of silence.
They wrestle grace from the turning of their green world to towers of ash.

Neighbours (on Marshall Street)

SANDY SHREVE

We discover each other slowly, through
summer afternoons renovating our houses,
hear histories between hammer strokes —
whose place used to be whose,
the school behind the transit line
once a dairy farm,
our urban lots the hayfield
until it burned.

Newcomers and old timers are introduced,
grow comfortable with people
who never would have cared to meet
if they hadn't chanced on the same block.

We say the same
about most relatives, co-workers.
If not for blood or job ties
we'd have nothing in common,
let the comment pass as if it's a given,
as if proof exists in how easily we lose touch
when we move on —
though they change us forever,
and we, them.

A citied-in street slows
the hurry-home from errands
with the syrup of blackberry scent and sweet peas
urging us back toward something
of the country town,
a craving for everyone to know everyone,
what we've been up to.

Fences eventually become supports to lean words on,
porches a reason to pause,
as we become neighbours for a season,
stitching together the remnants of a village
before winter sets in.

El Dorado: Champlain Heights

PAM GALLOWAY

Three birches make a triangle, perfectly
straight lines. The boy's feet mapped
twenty-four paces between them,
a scar on each trunk.

Now, he's down four feet and going,
blade striking stones, solid ground,
jolts jag through his wrists, his jaw tightens.
Breathless, he stops,
looks up to answer me.

Yes, treasure — inside these straggling tracts
of woodland behind the housing co-op,
under the cans, the plastic milk jugs
and a rusted, sad-eyed rocking horse —
all kinds of treasure is buried,
when you're young enough,
you want to spend each day
going tree to tree looking
for signs.

The gold will be his.
For twenty chocolate bars
a day, for his mother's face
when he tells her, We're rich
mum, we're rich. Let's order in.

Ridgeway:
commuting on two wheels

DAVID R. CONN

It's a rush out of 29th Avenue station,
hurtling down Earles to cross Kingsway,
turning west into mellow afternoon.
You pass baseball games in the parks,
homeowners pruning in shady yards.

Ridgeway undulates through the east end;
so you climb hard, then dip again.
Sprinting between traffic lights,
catch your breath waiting at the crossings.
Accelerate as crowds recede in peripheral vision.

[In a dream, the body also rides
but weightlessly, tirelessly,
legs pistoning, toying with balance;
skidding, pirouetting.
You don't need a machine.]

There's another rise at Prince Edward,
a mountain glimpse you've earned.
Then downhill, peeling off Ridgeway
for home; body charged, euphoric,
the daily commute an accomplishment.

1 a.m. this road, this way

MICHAEL TURNER

1 a.m. this road, this way
diagonal, in opposition
2 the grid, the monarchy
of streets: Beatrice, Sophia
3 princes, Earles, a Duchess, lords
& ladies waiting at
45 degrees with soldiers, explorers
businessmen, saints
6 places in Australia, a Salish
name that means "people of many names" from
7th to 10th Avenues, indefinitely
a taxi driver drives the whole
8 miles with a carload
of offshore investors
9 times before giving up
looking for the historic Gladstone Inn
10 hours later swerving to
avoid a fallen man sleeping off

The vernacular market isn't found on the tourist map, though the arrow pointing down at the intersection of Main and 49th street states "Punjabi Market"

KULDIP GILL

Betis (daughters) and bhenjis (sisters) hear the cry,
Come buy sari's, come buy our choli's,
Come buy, come buy
Petticoats, chunis, salvar/kamiz's,
Bangles, and bracelets,
Surma and mehndis
Bindi's and nose rings,
Creams to whiten your skin,
Or try threaded bow-like eyebrows
Come buy, come buy!
How shy she looks, her mother frowns,
But bhenjis know the sheers are fine
They twirl to see the lengha's line,
Oh, bhenji, make it mine, make it mine.
Together the beti and bhanji aspire
Add it to the bill, they whisper
And conspire to the merchant's
Cries: Come buy, Come buy!

Come buy! Come buy! The windows scream
The same dollars for two of anything.
Hindu videos, stock of best English-Punjabi dictionary,
New brass images of gods and goddesses.
In the Guru ka Bazaar, come buy, come buy
Gifts to the hundreds of wedding guests
In the beti's dowry — a crown for her husband;
The bride's home appliances. Come buy!
In gold jewelry shops — more per block than anywhere,
Bracelets and jewelled everythings. Come buy, come buy
Our Indian groceries. Garlic, ginger, heaps of eggplant,
Capsicum, okra, mustard greens and cauliflower. Come smell
the lentil and buy our spicy chai. Come buy our golden sweets,
Burfi's flavoured pistachio, peppered cashews, almond, figs. Come buy,
Come buy! Star fruit, ginger root. Come buy, come buy your daughter's
Pots and pans, lunch boxes for her children, Main and 49th:
A bazaar, a *cirque du soleil* of sound and smell.
Come buy in the Punjabi vernacular, Hindi,
Urdu, Tamil, Telegu, Tagalog,
Fiji-bat, Italian, Greek,
Mandarin and any other. Come buy!
Come buy! Come buy! At our Punjabi Market!

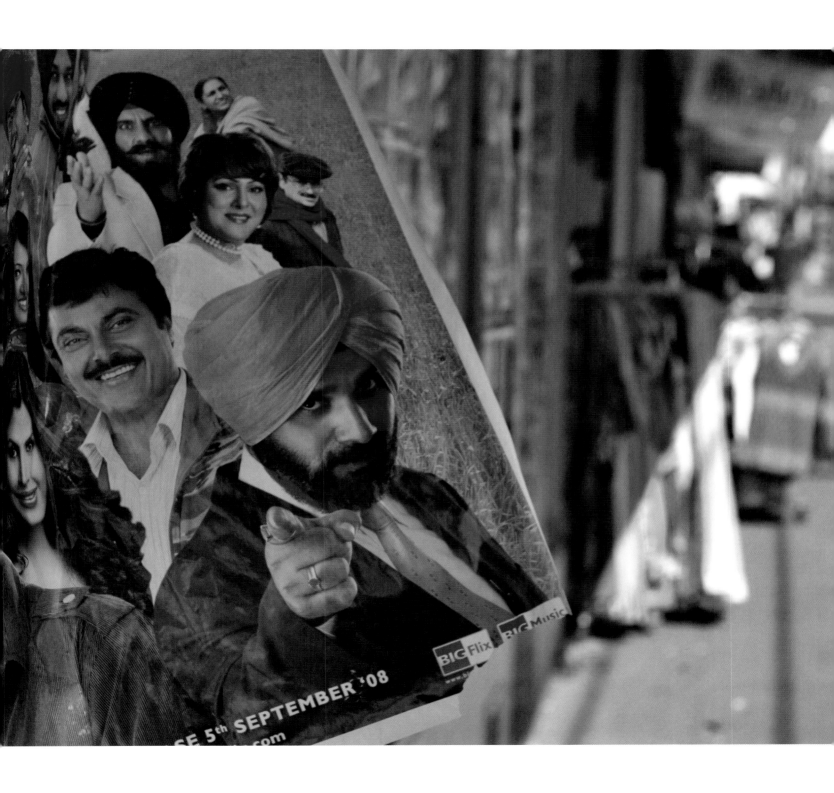

Gravity of the situation: stuck in the elevator of the Lee Building

HEIDI GRECO

nothing we can do but wait
inside this dangling box, stuck
between these floors that mutter
stories that no longer matter

the billboard on the roof continues
showing its jaded face
selling something nobody needs
to another Friday night
worn as any hooker
standing outside by the bus
hoping for some trick that might break
the beat of the evening's rain
    (all of us wish we'd thought to bring wine
    a bag of fatty snacks to help pass the time)

hanging by these dusty cables
closer to heaven than any of us wish,
holding on by breath of angels or worse,
I picture the rooftop billboard turning

some key for an antique wind-up toy
imagine it cranking us downward so slow
a cradle as soft as the crumbled clay
that lines the walls of this building. I wait
for the wakening rumble, beating heart of the ancient beast:
the tired machine that will grind its gears, manoeuvring
pulleys, shifting old weights. think of how it will groan
as it places us where we belong. the way we will step out
    onto the light-slicked surface of rained-on streets
    how we will walk away as if nothing has happened.

happy birthday dear house

JOY KOGAWA

happy birthday
dear house

born-again house
dream-come-true house
love-that-endures house
once-upon-a-time house
Momotaro-come-home house
I-love-everyone house

Marpole house

as the heart flies
straight home
home

full-throated
winds of mystery
white cherry blossoming
in the lane
mama's pure
soprano voice
in the land of mercy
in the land
of the second chance

Sestina for Shaughnessy

GENNI GUNN

I'd like to chug and glide a train
up the rise into the gravity of Shaughnessy, angle
around the curves of Angus Drive, the slopes
of Lilliputian meadows — the green of sky,
feed ravens from an open window
and ride a CPR train into the past

before the concrete, the million-dollar faces, past
memory's blockades. I'd like to ride a railway-baron train
lounge in a dining car and trace through velvet-curtained windows
the half-moon bays of Marguerite, angle
caboose past hedgerows, gaudy dancers, cedar sky,
the luscious dips and slopes

of topiary beasts and yews that edge the slopes
I'd like to whistle-blow a locomotion past
gates and motion sensors, barrelling through split, sky-
blue pools and invisible fences. I'd like to steer a cardinal train
through trespass laws and undulating angles,
hands grasping willows weeping into ponds outside the window,

elegant geometry, banks and arcs reflected in the window's
placid lake. I'd like to tumble-down a lexiscape of slopes,
the stagger joints and rock-offs, curl around angles
in degrees, on tangent tracks, steep gradients past
crossovers, turnouts and corridors of train-
ghosts lingering in the terminal between earth and sky

pink magnolias, birds in flight, the stippled sky,
a backdrop, marble and stone and shuttered windows,
the air itself purified. I'd like to ram a train
through porticos and granite lives, through market slopes
and slides down an embankment past
the manicured facades of Hosner, Nanton, Pine, angle

across sentinel displays, stacked railway ties angling
the landscape. Steel banding rips into a guillotine sky,
stakes drop, turnabouts cog past
spires and chimneys, cupolas, bay windows,
columns and arches, wrought iron gates and copper slopes
of roofs. I'd like to tunnel drive a train

metal on metal, the past a siding track, a train
angled into a cutting camellia sky,
the screech of brakes, the open window, the violet slopes.

Across the street

DIANE SUTHERLAND

Three houses in a row
all empty
mansions in fact
grand hollow mansions with hardwood floors
and leaded windows blank in the sunlight.
Offshore Owners say those who know.
Sometimes a light shines, but
no children ever play in the huge yards,
derelict lawns full of weeds,
trees that never feel any sharp cuts.
On a spring night we are wakened and
lie stilled by the throaty chorus of something
wild and wilful on the front lawn of our house.

Come summer it seems there are new neighbours
across the street,
a whole family, in fact,
at dusk we heard barking, and
barefoot on the still warm walk
I went to see what,
daring the shadows of the road
to pass to the other side
to peer over the gate into the drive
of that big house —
when in a sudden moonlit moment,
spilling out from the middle of the hedge,
skipping onto the pavement
came three, no four, no five
puppies.
Coyote children filling the yard.

Autumn, VanDusen Gardens

MICHAEL BULLOCK

Autumn has laid its chill finger on the gardens
curling the leaves
drowning the waterlilies
beneath cold brown water

The flowers are shrinking
back into their roots

The distant mountains
veil their sad faces
behind a scarf of mist

The ducks
cut arrowheads of ripples
that point away
toward some distant land

The sky reflects the darkness of the water
capping the garden
beneath a lid of gloom

Where it falls over the rocks
the water
has the whiteness of future snow

A single small tree
amid sere brown and yellow
glows with a crimson light

November

MICHAEL BULLOCK

Captured in ice
the waterlily leaves
hold their breath
and wait for spring

The ice bares its teeth
that glint
in the cold sun

57th and Oak

RENEE NORMAN

how those girls must have dreamed
soaring above their bodies
the stranger growing in their womb
a constant reminder
shame, regret, pain
the hallmarks of decency
hydrangeas and sturdy oaks
surrounding this house of reluctant mothers
this intersection of broken beginnings

and now my mother mindless
plucks a flower as she walks the path
along this same house transformed
rooms full of strangers
this house of lost memory
this place of endings
this sad intersection

grey on grey
(a view from Cambie Bridge)

DANIELA BOUNEVA ELZA

light filters through   the fog
grey on grey   the distances

between us   filled with
lost   glances

drizzle over   the inlet
city   hugging

the water tight   grey mist
fading   a jacket's bright colours

on the bridge   its thick   pillars
concrete   steel   seagulls

water   a thirty floor scraper of sky
in front of   rushing   pewter

clouds   in a grey like that
it is motion   that sets us apart

Black Dog survives

TANA RUNYAN

Each morning the jackhammer's pneumatic jabber,
dusty miasma of backhoes, earth movers, dump trucks.
One block away an asthmatic child reaches for his puffer
as the cut that is not yet covered deepens, bisects
the neighbourhood. The seven-storey trench disappears
downhill into the tunnel where Costa Rican excavators
kneel at candlelit shrines; Santa Barbara, their red-robed
guardian, keeper of those who risk sudden explosive death.
Noise at eighty decibels, concrete barriers, chain-link fences
sever storefronts from foot traffic too annoyed to Shop the Line.

Abby moves to Fort Langley. Don-Don is squeezed, then gone.
Om, its lotus root and taro dishes, folds in upon itself. Tomato
goes west, along with Kestrel and the literary cat, Ruby.
Hazel's window demands compensation but the Falcon tells
shopkeepers to get over it, that businesses will come and businesses
will go. Black Dog survives. One Tooth survives. Bob still hawks
the Street Corner outside Choices. Perhaps the florist will sell a tuberose.
Theresa's mural of faces smiles down from the Cambie General Store.
At night the locals venture out, eat red Thai curry, jambalaya, lemon crepes,
pho', nasi goreng and coconut buns. A handful watch a foreign film
in the theatre whose lovers' seats boast lumbar support. Many more gather
to drink sangria and listen to *flamenco puro*. The *cantaora* lays down
her lament. The dancer's heels pound out their defiant *zapateado*.
This other rhythm seeps into the sidewalk as her hands form the bull's
horns above her magnificent dark head and the clapping begins.

Little Mountain

LIONEL KEARNS

Someone is singing in the park,
full round syllables filling up
the emptiness. He walks quickly,
singing O *Sole Mio*, leaving
as a sign of his absence this
small patch of balanced stillness.
The curved sky in the west
is a pale memory of day. Street lights
flicker on, and traffic murmur
cancels out another distinct moment.

Down one at The Nat

Through these windows comes the breath of the world
- from "Ode to Sadness" by Pablo Neruda

ROB TAYLOR

The ballpark shines,
this blue world an ode
to Neruda's odes —
newsprint
and baseball
caps, salty socks
and watermelon
grins — the glistenings
of summer.

The pitcher bows,
bat ripples, white ball
bounces into the
artichoke-
green outfield, nestles
in its gloved heart.

The red earth
before second base springs
up, dugouts clear —
the finely ironed
infield trampled
under glinting spikes.

We stand as one,
wave in the breeze,
spit black
watermelon-seed
words
which spill
like beautiful tears
over this city.

Nights above Fraser Street

JENNICA HARPER

One way, there are yellow lights, like
forest eyes, reflected in thick black water.
The other way slopes up and up,
lit by white lampfog and video store neon.
The number 8 bus sparks and sizzles,
casting fat shadows on a short man
carrying a baseball bat like an umbrella.
A police car cruises a slow patrol. Same one,
three times. Long-legged women dressed
in silver and black, hair pulled back tight,
are hard as rock and bone, shivering.

The woman next door leans out her open window
wearing a hat and gloves; her copper-tipped
cigarette draws loops in the air in front of her.
She has never noticed me. She spells out
her name, her address, tomorrow's
to-do list, with her fire and smoke.
She tips ash ceremoniously into a coffee can.
Language, like fire, is a discovery —
not an invention. Night upon night, the woman sits
and lets particles of dust, words, spill
through the open frame of my glass,
and in this way, we talk.

Harriet Street

CAMERON JOHNSON

2 blocks, maybe 30 houses
between 28th and 30th.
Harriet Street. The smallest, it seems, in Vancouver.
Cab drivers don't know it. I give the address, idling
in front of the domestic terminal, and
the driver repeats a litany: "Harriet? Harriet. Harriet." He tastes
the street, but he — master of roadways, navigator of asphalt — does not
know it. I have a map.
"Near Fraser and 30th," I say, and — magic words being spoken — the
cab begins to move.
I move into the house on Halloween.
My first memories:
cardboard boxes, unfamiliar smells of tenants past,
pumpkins, pizza in the middle of an empty living room,
candy and Superman costumes.
The children (there are many on Harriet Street)
know each other, and under the darkening sky,
run up to doors and accept candy — not from strangers.
This is Harriet, and parents stand unconcerned in the road, and children
race the sidewalks, holding hands when they cross the street.
I watch, sitting on a stack of boxes containing dusty paperbacks with ripped covers.
To the south, Harriet ends. A house blocks
its way.
To the north, Harriet becomes an alley, anemic and rough,
populated with recycling bins and gravel.
An old man sweeping his driveway told me
this is one of the oldest neighbourhoods in the city
and I believe him. (My home was built in 1923. It's
over 80 years old.)
80 years. 30 homes. 2 blocks.

Pacific Spirit Park

ANNELIESE SCHULTZ
for Max Approaching 10

Every step from shade to sun and back,

each rush of creek

or roundelay of hidden birds,

each rainbow'd spider web

and every slash of light 'cross needled path,

I count as unexpected gift —

Just like each sudden laugh,

like every lone or well-loved dog I see,

like windy nights,

like seven messages,

or like the part of you that's just like me,

the part that's not.

Maple Grove Park

MAVIS JONES

On a cool July day three figures
under the trees move with the slow
gestures of tai chi, as if they were forming a sutra.
Some crows in a more martial mode
chastise with rough voices a solitary jogger.
At the end of a pink leash, a dog pulls
his attendant along, barely remembering
the wild packs he once followed, undomesticated,
fierce. They circle a birthday party of three-year-olds,
lemonade, cookies, and a swaying cluster
of bright balloons, flowers in this unwatered garden.

An uninterrupted rain forest dwelt here
more than a hundred years ago.
It blows in the wind from the sea, the rain
from the blue mountains, speaks
in brushing leaves of maples, fronds of cedar,
thin growth of Douglas fir. In the dimness under,
slowly decaying stumps of old trees,
massive and grey, sit like ancient dwarfs.
Children climb on their flat logged tops,
hide within a hollowed-out trunk,
and wonder why the treetops disappeared.
Like the dog, we have left behind
a fiercer place, wolves, deer, bear,
the river full of salmon. Only the stumps
and the urban coyotes at night remind us,
and the children, who own this last remnant
of that shining world.

Then: map of the city

LAISHA ROSNAU

He was the Number 14, a bus ride
down Hastings one way, strung
with blinking lights and sparks
of trolleys unhooked, headed
to Arbutus, the salt lick of ocean,
tongues swollen to lap up the whole thing.

He was a drum kit under the full skirt
of a tree, rain trenched around it.
Kicked out of a cab near Lost Lagoon,
he was a cedar thick enough
to keep the drum's skin dry and tight,
a snared lullaby before sleep.

He was chain-links around the marina,
winches loosed by wind, rigging
played against spar and mast like chimes
frothed into a frenzy. He was the mainstay
snapped and boom slammed into the dock,
light splintered on black water.

He was the underside of Cambie Street Bridge,
algae barnacled lace on pilings, twisted
salal of fire growing out of a barrel, boys
playing basketball, steady ring of rubber
against pavement echoed off False Creek,
a watered down version of tides.

He was a billboard crowning a brick building
on Main and Broadway, images of thirst
unsated on the outside, inside a keyhole
in a metal door, wooden staircase, space
between signs. He was murmur of rock doves,
lights weaving the mountains into a nest.

Airport music

MARITA DACHSEL
(after Charles Baxter)

We have over-packed again.
The straps already straining our shoulders,
our lower backs already tiring to the weight
and we are only in the airport.

We haven't checked in yet, but are standing
at the concourse window, coffees in hand,
watching the take-offs,
                                        the arrivals.
(Those flying tins full
of expectancy.)

We know we could put the packs down,
save our bodies, but somehow that would feel like cheating.

We are silently listening for it.

                                        We can't hear it,
but we feel it — that airport music — a pop tune
that never leaves us,
                                        infecting,
                                        humming
inside for so long that we can't tell the difference
between it and our own beating hearts.

We have been on many trips without the other,
but now that seems inconceivable.
                                        Why
would I venture anywhere without you —
my perfect travelling partner,
                                        my journeying companion?

I am here and I want to take your hand,
but I don't. There is no need to.
You know I am here. We are ready to go.

ACKNOWLEDGEMENTS

Jancis Andrews, "Grandmothers in Chinatown" © Jancis Andrews, by permission of the author; Oana Avasilichioaei, "Museum" from *feria*, Wolsak & Wynn © 2008, by permission of the author; Elizabeth Bachinsky, "On the death of the Lions Gate Bridge" © Elizabeth Bachinsky, by permission of the author; Daniela Bouneva Elza, "A walk down apostrophe lane" and "grey on grey" © Daniela Bouneva Elza, by permission of the author; Stephanie Bolster, "Terminal" © Stephanie Bolster, by permission of the author; Lillian Boraks-Nemetz, "A kiss in Nitobe Garden" © Lillian Boraks-Nemetz, by permission of the author; Kate Braid, "Union welders: overtime" from *Covering Rough Ground*, Polestar Book Publishers, © Kate Braid 1991, by permission of the author; Brian Brett, "Crabs under Second Narrows Bridge" from *Smoke Without Exit*, Sono Nis Press, © Brian Brett 1984, by permission of the author; Michael Bullock, "Autumn: VanDusen Gardens" and "November:" from *Vancouver Moods*, Third Eye © 1989, by permission of Lori-ann Latremouille and the Michael Bullock estate; Trevor Carolan, "What Jack Shadbolt said" © Trevor Carolan, by permission of the author; Mark Cochrane, "Point Grey, Saturday paper" © Mark Cochrane, by permission of the author; David Conn, "Ridgeway: commuting on two wheels" © David Conn, by permission of the author; Marita Dachsel, "Airport music" from *All Things Said & Done*, Caitlin Press © 2007, by permission of the author; Andrea Dancer, "Erasure at Westcoast Tattoo" © Andrea Dancer, by permission of the author; John Donlan, "Babies' Cottage" © John Donlan, by permission of the author; Joseph Ferone, "BC Collateral" © Joseph Ferone, by permission of the author; George Fetherling, "The Sylvia" © George Fetherling, by permission of the author; Pam Galloway, "Sun Yat-Sen's garden" and "El Dorado" © Pam Galloway, by permission of the author; Zsuzsi Gartner, "Wreck(ed) Beach, 1997" © Zsuzsi Gartner, by permission of the author; Gary Geddes, "Active trading" © Gary Geddes, by permission of the author; Jennifer S. Getsinger, "Kitsilano is not Nantucket, though" © Jennifer S. Getsinger, by permission of the author; Kuldip Gill, "Punjabi Market" © Kuldip Gill, by permission of the author; Genni Gunn, "Sestina for Shaughnessy" © Genni Gunn, by permission of the author; Heidi Greco, "Gravity of the situation: stuck in the elevator of the Lee Building" © Heidi Greco, by permission of the author; Heather Haley, "Whore in the eddy" © Heather Haley, by permission of the author; Jennica Harper, "Nights above Fraser Street" from *The Octopus and Other Poems*, Signature Editions © 2006, by permission of the author; Mark Harris, "The town is just so damned rational" © Mark Harris, by permission of the author; Wes Hartley, "Kitsilano Point ghost muskrat swamp" © Wes Hartley, by permission of the author; Aislinn Hunter, "Under Christchurch bells" from *Into the Early Hours*, Polestar, © Aislinn Hunter 2001, by permission of the author; Chris Hutchinson, "The man who lives in the gazebo" © Chris Hutchinson, by permission of the author; Maureen Hynes, "Heronry" © Maureen Hynes, by permission of the author; Cameron Johnson, "Harriet Street" © Cameron Johnson, by permission of the author; Mavis Jones, "Maple Grove Park" © Mavis Jones, by permission of the author; Lionel Kearns, "Little Mountain" and "Vancouver General" © Lionel Kearns, by permission of the author; Joy Kogawa, "happy birthday dear house" © Joy Kogawa, by permission of the author; Fiona Tinwei Lam, "Vanier Park" © Fiona Tinwei Lam, by permission of the author; Evelyn Lau, "Quayside" © Evelyn Lau, by permission of the author; Clinton John Leon, "Gulls (Granville Island)" and "Seal at English Bay" © Clinton John Leon, by permission of the author; Christopher Levenson, "Listening in" © Christopher Levenson, by permission of the author; Bernice Lever, "Words on the streets" © Bernice Lever, by permission of the author; Pat Lowther, "Vancity" from *Final Instructions*, West Coast Review/Orca Sound © 1980, by permission of Beth and Christine Lowther; Justin Lukyn, "002864" from *Henry Pepper*, New Star Books © 2008, by permission of author; George McWhirter, "Where Kits sits" from *The Incorrection*, Oolichan Books © 2007, by permission of the author; Daphne Marlatt, "Moonshine" © Daphne Marlatt, by permission of the author; Roy Miki, "There are some days" © Roy Miki, by permission of the author; William H. New, "my vancouver starts" from *Touching Ecuador*, Oolichan Books © 2006 , by permission of the author; Renee Norman, "57th & Oak" © Renee Norman, by permission of the author; Bud Osborn, "Jackson avenue and *east* hastings" from *hundred block rock*, Arsenal Pulp Press © 1999, by permission of the author; Catherine Owen, "Alleyway, 8 a.m." from *Shall*, Wolsak & Wynn © 2006, by permission of the author; José Emilio Pacheco, "Musqueam" from *The Selected Poems of José Emilio Pacheco*, New Directions Publishing Inc. © George McWhirter 1987, by permission of the translator and the original author; Barbara Pelman, "Sam's Shirt Shop on Hastings" © Barbara Pelman, by permission of the author; Lynda Grace Philippsen, "Happy Hour: Bacchus Lounge" © Lynda Grace Philippsen, by permission of the author; Goh Poh Seng, "Evening on Victoria" © Goh Poh Seng, by permission of the author; Al Purdy, "Piling Blood" from *The Collected Poems of Al Purdy*, Harbour Publishing © 2000, by permission of Harbour Publishing and Eurithe Purdy; Meredith Quartermain, "Cathedral" from *Walking Vancouver*, NeWest Press © 2005, "Scaffolding" from *Nightmarker*, NeWest Press © 2008, by permission of the author; Linda Rogers, "Everything but horses" © Linda Rogers, by permission of the author; Laisha Rosnau, "Then: map of the city" © Laisha Rosnau, by permission of the author; Tana Runyan, "Black Dog survives" © Tana Runyan, by permission of the author; Allan Safarik, "Fish candy" © Allan Safarik, by permission of the author; Maria Sammarco, "Meals on Wheels, nineteen eighty-eight" © Maria Sammarco, by permission of the author; Karoly Sandor, "Quinte (Goddess on Tenth Avenue) © Karoly Sandor, by permission of the author; Anneliese Schultz, "Pacific Spirit Park" © Anneliese Schultz, by permission of the author; Sandy Shreve, "Neighbours (on Marshall Street)" © Sandy Shreve, by permission of the author; Christine Schrum, "Purgatory" © Christine Schrum, by permission of the author; Ron Smith, "The fourth moon of Broadway" © Ron Smith, by permission of the author; Madeline Sonik, "Gage Tower" © Madeline Sonik, by permission of the author; George Stanley, "Fire alarm" from *Vancouver: A Poem*, New Star Books © 2008, by permission of the author; Wayne Stedingh, "4:00 a.m." © Wayne Stedingh, by permission of the author; Shannon Stewart, "December aquarium" © Shannon Stewart, by permission of the author; Diane Sutherland, "Silver thaw" and "Across the street" © Diane Sutherland, by permission of the author; Madeleine Thien, "SkyTrain: Main and Terminal, 1983" © Madeleine Thien, by permission of the author; Russell Thornton, "When the big hand is on the starfish" © Russell Thornton, by permission of the author; Leslie Timmins, "Where the numbers meet the trees" © Leslie Timmins, by permission of the author; Bibiana Tomasic, "99 Express — 8 a.m." © Bibiana Tomasic, by permission of the author; Diane Tucker, "The crows cope" © Diane Tucker, by permission of the author; Michael Turner, "1 a.m. this road, this way" from *Kingsway*, Arsenal Pulp Press © 1995, by permission of the author; Julia van Gorder, "Seawall: Stanley Park" and "The poet with stones has moved" © Julia van Gorder, by permission of the author; David Watmough, "Kits Pool" from *Coming down the Pike*, Ekstasis Editions © 2008, by permission of the author; Tom Wayman, "Sea wrack" © Tom Wayman, by permission of the author; Zachariah Wells, "Leg in Boot Square" © Zachariah Wells, by permission of the author; George Whipple, "Seabus" © George Whipple, by permission of the author; Gudrun Will, "Date stamp" © Gudrun Will, by permission of the author; Rita Wong, "take a st. and" © Rita Wong, by permission of the author; Jim Wong-Chu, "pender street east" and "curtain of rain" © Jim Wong-Chu, by permission of the author; George Woodcock, "The cherry tree on Cherry Street" from *The Cherry Tree on Cherry Street*, Quarry Press, © George Woodcock, by permission of The Writers' Trust of Canada.

CONTRIBUTORS

Jancis M. Andrews, winner of The *Vancouver Sun* 1992 poetry contest, is best known as an outspoken activist for human rights and for her two books of stories: *Rapunzel, Rapunzel, Let Down Your Hair* and *Walking on Water*.

Oana Avasilichioaei has lived in Vancouver for twelve years. Her recent book, *feria: A Poempark* (Wolsak & Wynn, 2008) frolics through fractured histories of Hastings Park.

Elizabeth Bachinsky moved lately from the Fraser Valley to the Hastings Sunrise area, near the docks, among the abattoirs, in East Vancouver. Nightwood Editions follows her 2006 Governor-General's-Award-nominated *Home of Sudden Service* with *God of Missed Connections*, 2009.

Stephanie Bolster was born in Vancouver and raised in Burnaby, and although she now lives in Montreal she often visits her parents at her childhood address. 1998 Governor General's award winner and the editor of *The Best Canadian Poetry in English 2008* (Tightrope).

Lillian Boraks-Nemetz is an author of poetry and fiction. She has recently read her poems in a documentary entitled *Poetry of Resilience*, filmed at UBC's Nitobe Memorial Garden and in Europe.

Daniela Bouneva Elza listens to the languages spoken by people, trees, and crows between the mountains, bridges, and waters of Vancouver. Daniela has poems forthcoming in *Poetic Inquiry* and *Van Gogh's Ear*.

Kate Braid, born in Calgary, raised in Montreal and schooled in Sackville, New Brunswick, found her home in 1970 when she met the cedar trees in Stanley Park. Her latest publication is *A Well-Mannered Storm: The Glenn Gould Poems* (Caitlin, 2008).

Brian Brett, an east end child, was born in Vancouver General Hospital in 1950. Author of ten books of poetry, fiction and memoir, and journalism for Canada's major newspapers, Brett's *Trauma Farm: A Natural Living History of Living on the Land*, will be released by Greystone Books this fall.

Michael Bullock, who died in 2008, was the last of the British surrealist group associated with Sir Herbert Read. Poet and painter, lover of gardens, Michael Bullock moved to Vancouver from London, England, in 1968 and made it his home for forty years.

Trevor Carolan has lived in the Vancouver area since 1957. "BC's literary jack of all trades" (*Quill & Quire*), he teaches English at the University of the Fraser Valley.

Mark Cochrane is a Vancouver Quadra constituent from west of Alma. His poem "Eskimo Rescue" — about kayaking in English Bay — appears in the Spring 2009 issue of *The Malahat Review*.

David R. Conn, a librarian and writer, often uses the Vancouver bikeways. He reviews environmental books and DVDs for *Library Journal*.

Marita Dachsel now lives in Edmonton. During her twelve years in Vancouver, she became writer, wife, and mother. Her book of verse, *All Things Said & Done* (Caitlin Press, 2007), was shortlisted for the ReLit Award.

Andrea Dancer, a Vancouverite since 1972, has never relinquished the bohemianism that defined Vancouver then. She now lives, listens, and writes between a cabin in the Gulf Islands and a seventeenth-century farmhouse in the Bohemian-Moravian Highlands of the Czech Republic.

John Donlan is a reference librarian at Vancouver Public Library. His latest book is *Spirit Engine*, from Brick Books.

Joseph Ferone, best known for his recorded songs, his novel *Boomboom*, and his musical, *Harbour Light*, with CBC Radio, is assembling his 1960s street poems in a book. Former longshoreman, tugboat hand, Arctic construction worker, merchant seaman, and photojournalist, he lives in Vancouver's Hastings-Sunrise area.

George Fetherling moved to BC in 2001. By that time he had already, for over thirty-some years, resided in the province for periods long and short. Vancouver is at the centre of his novel *Jericho* (Random House, 2005).

Maxine Gadd lives in the Downtown Eastside, Vancouver: a sidewalk oracle, speaking for her generation and the evolution of her cosmos in the city. An excerpt from 'Maxine Meets Proteus in Gastown,' from *Backup to Babylon* (New Star) rode the Vancouver buses with the Poetry in Transit project, 2007.

Pam Galloway, originally from Manchester, England, is a trained speech therapist who has lived in Vancouver for the past twenty-three years. Her most recent book of verse, *Parallel Lines*, is from Ekstasis Editions.

Zsuzsi Gartner is author of *All The Anxious Girls on Earth* and editor of the upcoming *Darwin's Bastards*, Canadian fiction about the near-future. She arrived in Vancouver in 1990 via Calgary, Ottawa and Toronto and has preserved her love/hate relationship with the burg ever since.

Gary Geddes, although he lives in Victoria now, was born in Vancouver and raised in the portentous surroundings of "Active Trading". *Falsework*, his latest book-length poem, is on the disastrous collapse of the Second Narrows Bridge.

Jennifer S. Getsinger, literary geologist and editor, came to Vancouver from the US in 1979. She lives in Kitsilano, "not Nantucket", and her poem alludes to a whale of a vanished weathervane atop one of Kits' houses. She has read at SFU's Writers' Studio.

Heidi Greco says her too-comfortable South Surrey house and cuts in transit have diminished her link to Vancouver. Appearing in *Crossing Lines* (Seraphim Editions, 2008), the anthology of poetry by US citizens who came to Canada in the Vietnam War era, marked an historic and emotional milestone for her.

Kuldip Gill, born in the Punjab and raised in the Fraser Valley, recently returned from Vancouver to her childhood home in Mission. Past president of Immigrant and Visible Minority Women of BC, she has a PhD in Anthropology and a BC Book Prize for her *Dharma Rasa* (Nightwood, 2000).

Genni Gunn says "Vancouver is the home I long for when I'm away." She translates from and is translated into Italian, her first language. Genni's latest poetry collection is *Faceless* (Signature Editions, 2007).

Heather Haley has inhabited the MetroVan area since 1979. Her *Window Seat and Sideways* was published by Anvil in 2003. *Princess Nut* by AURAL Heather, is a CD of spoken word songs from RPW Records released in June 2008.

Jennica Harper came to Vancouver from Toronto in 1998. She lives near Fraser & East 11th, technically, in Mount Pleasant, and on the way to the graveyard at 41st. Her *What It Feels Like For a Girl* was released by Anvil Press in 2007.

Mark Harris, a prize-winning playwright, is a major contributor to an upcoming monograph on BC's most politically-committed documentary filmmaker, Nettie Wild. Also a poet, writer, critic and translator, he teaches Film Studies at the University of British Columbia.

Wes Hartley, known locally as Kitsilano Wes, has written twenty-one books in various genres over forty-five-plus years, eleven of poetry. Most recently, *Sterile Hybrids* and *Cat of the Islands: Selected Poems*, both from WH Editions.

Aislinn Hunter is a poet and novelist who currently divides her time between Vancouver and Edinburgh. In the fall of 2008 she was Writer-in-Residence at Memorial University in St John's, Newfoundland. Her most recent collection is *The Possible Past* (Polestar).

Chris Hutchinson is from Arizona and writes about a man who lives in a Vancouver gazebo. His verse titles are *Unfamiliar Weather* (Muses' Company, 2005) and *Other People's Lives* (Brick Books, 2009).

Maureen Hynes, a winner of the Gerald Lampert and the Petra Kenney Poetry Awards, visits Vancouver and its heronry, frequently. Her most recent volume is *Harm's Way* (Brick Books).

Cameron Johnson, editor at NUVO magazine, has lived in or near Vancouver all his life and particularly enjoys the lively coffee haunts on Main.

Mavis Jones grew up on the coast north of Vancouver. She came to the city to attend the University of British Columbia. "Shallal", published in Laurie Ricou's compendium on *Salal*, speaks to her relationship with the city/wilderness landscape.

Lionel Kearns has lived in Vancouver for half a century — off Commercial Drive, now, facing the North Shore mountains. His poems have recently ridden the eye-line ad-panels of Vancouver buses with Poetry in Transit.

Joy Kogawa Born in Vancouver, 1935, her novel *Obasan* was a One Book One Vancouver choice, and Vancouver Opera produced her *Naomi's Road*. The Marpole house she grew up in was purchased by the Land Conservancy of BC. *The Literary Review of Canada* has her latest poem.

Fiona Tinwei Lam, a Vancouverite since age four, is the author of *Intimate Distances*. Her latest book, *Enter the Chrysanthemum*, is from Caitlin Press, 2009.

Evelyn Lau was born in Vancouver in 1971 and now makes her home in Yaletown. Author of nine books of prose and poetry, her most recent verse is *Treble* (Raincoast).

C. J. Leon moved to Vancouver in 2006 after completing his Hon. BSc. in mathematics at the University of Toronto. Composer of verses and classical guitar, his latest EP, *Cold Clay*, was praised as low-fi high art and compared to "Early Leonard Cohen singing into a beer can on a $12 guitar" (Jeremiah Sutherland).

Christopher Levenson, after forty years in Ottawa, in August 2007, migrated with his wife, Oonagh, to the Vancouver oft-visited and beloved for its sea and mountains. Mother Tongue Publishing includes him in its anthology of contemporary BC verse, *Rocksalt*, 2008.

Bernice Lever, friend and foster-mother of Canadian poets, lives on Bowen Island. She is active with the North Vancouver Writers, World Poetry at the Vancouver Public Library, and Surrey Writers' Festival. Her *Never a Straight Line* (Black Moss) is a pocket-book poetry gem.

Pat Lowther's tragic death in 1975 deprived Vancouver of a great poet. *A Stone Diary* (Oxford, 1977) proved she was one of Canada's best. *Final Instructions* (West Coast Review/Orca Sound) is a posthumous collection. She was born in North Vancouver.

Justin Lukyn has lived in New York, San Francisco, Los Angeles, Boulder, Atlanta, Halifax, and for the past five years, East Van. *Henry Pepper* (New Star, 2008), centred on the Downtown Eastside, is his first poetry book.

Daphne Marlatt, Member of the Order of Canada, thinks of Vancouver as her "muse-city." In her narrative poem, *The Given* (McClelland & Stewart, 2008), the city is as present as the characters.

Roy Miki has lived close to Kits Beach in Kitsilano since he moved from Winnipeg in the late 60s. Member of the Order of Canada, Governor General's Award winner for *Surrender* (Mercury, 2002), Roy's most recent book of poems is *There* (New Star 2006).

William New was born in Vancouver and grew up on its South Slope. Returning from abroad in 1965, he lived in Kerrisdale, then further north in Kitsilano. His children's book, *The Year I Was Grounded* (2008), is his most recent. William is a Member of the Order of Canada.

Renee Norman's second book of poetry, *Backhand Through the Mother* (Inanna) will be followed by a third, *Martha in the Mirror*, Fall 2009. She is a professor at the University of the Fraser Valley, but still frequents Vancouver where she attended UBC.

Bud Osborn, Poet Laureate of the DTES, has lived in the Downtown Eastside of Vancouver for 20 years. Author of six poetry books, he appears in the anthology *Crossing Lines*, poetry by US citizens who came to Canada during the Vietnam War era.

Catherine Owen was born in Vancouver and lived there until 2006 when she moved to Edmonton. Her latest book is *Cusp/detritus: an experiment in alleyways* (Anvil, 2006).

José Emilio Pacheco has lived his life in the same house in Mexico City's Colonia Condesa. In the late sixties, he spent a year in Vancouver. Octavio Paz dubbed him "Dr. Pangloss in reverse." He is married to the TV journalist and writer Cristina Pacheco.

John Pass lives in the house he built on the Sunshine Coast. With his wife and writer, Theresa Kishkan, he runs High Ground Press. Since his sixties student days at UBC and job in the archives, Vancouver has been "the city" in his work. *Stumbling into Bloom* (2005), latest in the book series "At Large," won the Governor General's award for poetry in 2006.

Barbara Pelman was born in Vancouver, grew up "east of Oak," and graduated from the University of British Columbia. Her latest poetry book, *Borrowed Rooms*, was published by Ronsdale Press in 2008.

Lynda Grace Philippsen, a Metro Vancouver resident since 1971. She writes reviews for *The Globe and Mail* and *The Vancouver Sun*, and is a contributor to the book *Half in the Sun: Anthology of Mennonite Writing*.

Goh Poh Seng completed school and med studies in Ireland, spent twenty-five years practicing as a doctor and writer in his native Singapore, emigrated to Canada in 1986, requalified as an MD in Newfoundland, summered there and wintered in Vancouver. His verse has a trans-Canadian, universal appeal. *Asiaweek* calls him "a top-notch playwright, novelist and poet."

Al Purdy's poetry tapped the core of poetry common to Canadians. The League of Canadian Poets declared April 21, 2009 *National Al Purdy Day*. In the small cemetery at the end of Purdy Lane in Ameliasburg, Ontario, he lies near his A-frame, now the focus of a national campaign for its preservation.

Meredith Quartermain has been in Vancouver since 1972. Her most recent books are *Matter* (BookThug) and *Nightmarker* (NeWest).

Linda Rogers is Victoria's current Poet Laureate and granddaughter of Francis Trollope-Wilgress, the first male baby of European descent born in Vancouver. She grew up in the University Hill area and as a young wife moved to Southlands. Her next novel in The Empress Trilogy is *The Third Day Book*.

Laisha Rosnau wrote and published her first poetry collection and novel between bike rides in Vancouver. Prince George was home to the completion of her latest book, *Lousy Explorers*.

Tana Runyan lives where she writes, between Cambie and Main. She has been a member of the celebrated Vancouver writers' group, Sex, Death & Madness. Her first volume of verse is *Arithmetic of Surrender* from Exile Editions, 2007.

Allan Safarik grew up above the Burrard Inlet, where his family made its living off the fish and the water. Now, of Dundurn, Saskatchewan, his latest volume is *Yellowgrass*. He was editor of our city's centennial anthology, *Vancouver Poetry* (Polestar).

Maria Sammarco, architect and painter, hails from Italy and has lived in Vancouver since 1968. *Construction*, her five-month-long, inaugural installation marked the opening of Vancouver's new Central Public Library in 1995.

Karoly Sandor "A slave of your charms," he says, "(Vancouver) I fell in love with you." From Budapest in 1957 via Edmonton, Sandor has read his poems on CBC Radio and is a member of the Austin Closing Times literary group.

Christine Schrum, M.A., is a sometime Vancouverite. She recently co-edited *Leaves by Night, Flowers by Day* — an anthology of US poets including PEN/Faulkner-nominee Gladys Swann.

Anneliese Schultz An American immigrant to Vancouver by way of Italy, Anneliese teaches Italian at UBC. Her short play, "27 Years," was produced in 2007. Résumé and passionate outbursts can be found on Facebook.

Sandy Shreve writes of where she lives in Vancouver — the eastside, mainly — since 1971. She is godmother to the Vancouver buses' Poetry in Transit. *Suddenly, So Much* (Exile Editions, 2005) is her most recent volume.

Ron Smith was born in Vancouver and raised on the westside within earshot of the Easthopes, heading out from the Fraser into the strait — another mainland road. *Elf the Eagle*, his latest, is an illustrated book for children.

Madeline Sonik, now living in Victoria, sojourned in Kitsilano's 'Asthma Hollow' between Blenheim and MacDonald for her PhD in Education at UBC. Inanna released her first poetry book *Stone Sightings* in 2008.

George Stanley says Vancouver isn't really his city, but he has friends whose city it is, and he shares their love for it. Originally from San Francisco, his shared love for the city fills *Vancouver: A Poem* (New Star, 2008).

R.W. Stedingh, a Vancouver poet, arrived in the city from the US via Spain, where he studied flamenco guitar. He most recently appeared in *Queen's Quarterly, Descant, Canadian Literature* and the book, *Poems from the European Notebooks* (Lyre Press, 2001).

Shannon Stewart grew up on Vancouver's North Shore, a place she still calls home. Her most recent collection of poetry, *Penny Dreadful*, was published by Signal Editions in 2008.

Diane Sutherland, second-generation, Vancouver-born writer, seeks a publisher for *Season of Fever and Other Dawnings* by Ana Istaru — grand poet-diva of Costa Rica. Diane pays her bills selling real estate and plans on building a house in Mexico.

Rob Taylor, apart from following his partner to Africa, has spent his life in Vancouver, currently on Commercial Drive. Recent verse is in *The Antigonish Review, Dalhousie Review* and BC poet anthology, *Rocksalt: An Anthology of Contemporary BC Poetry*.

Madeleine Thien, a Vancouver girl, is a winner of the Ethel Wilson Prize and a City of Vancouver Book Prize for her fiction. This is her first published poem.

Russell Thornton has lived in several Vancouver neighbourhoods, currently, in North Vancouver. His most recent book is *The Human Shore*.

Leslie Timmins feels most at home along the shores of Burrard Inlet. Recently she has explored other edges in an essay about the poet-mentor relationship published in the journal *Other Voices*.

Bibiana Tomasic moved to Vancouver, aged eleven, from Zagreb, Croatia. As an adult, she took the 99 Express bus across town to attend classes at UBC. Her book of poems, *So Large an Animal*, is due from Leaf Press in the fall of 2009.

Diane Tucker, born and raised in the city, says that Vancouver is the home of her heart in this world. Circle your reading with her *Bright Scarves of Hours* (Palimpsest Press, 2007).

Michael Turner writes poetry, novels, screenplays, and non-fiction. His recent *Vancouver Photographs* with Fred Herzog (VAG/Douglas & McIntyre) was a 2008 City of Vancouver Book Prize nominee.

Julia van Gorder claims to reside in the sky — a highrise, next to the heronry in Stanley Park. Two of her poems recently made honourable mention in the Burnaby Writers' Competition.

David Watmough lived with his partner, the late Floyd St. Clair, on West 1st Avenue before moving to Tsawwassen. Renowned for his fiction, non-fiction, and monodramas, *Coming Down the Pike*, a book of sonnets with Ekstasis, is his debut volume of verse.

Tom Wayman, co-founder of the Vancouver Industrial Writers' Union and the Kootenay School of Writing's Vancouver Centre, co-edited *East of Main* — a best-selling 1989 verse anthology. Harbour Publishing released *High Speed Through Shoaling Water* in 2007.

Zachariah Wells would never have moved to Vancouver without his Vancouverite wife. His most recent book is *Anything But Hank!*, a verse story for children, co-written with Rachel Lebowitz and illustrated by Eric Orchard.

George Whipple, born in Saint John, NB, grew up in Toronto and now lives in Burnaby, writing, sketching, and translating French poetry. St. Thomas Book Series published *Swim Class* in 2008.

Gudrun Will edits *The Vancouver Review*. This is the first "found poem" taken from her writing in the magazine, and first published poem.

Rita Wong lives above Great Northern Way in Mount Pleasant. Her most recent books are *Sybil Unrest* (co-authored with Larissa Lai, Line Books 2008) and *forage* (Nightwood 2007).

Jim Wong-Chu, a founder of *Rice Paper* and the Asian Writers' Workshop, has been a postal worker, poet, and mentor to young writers in Vancouver. Born in Hong Kong, he was brought to Canada in 1953 as a "paper son" and raised by relatives in BC.

George Woodcock, until the time of his death in 1995, lived with his wife, Inge, for years on McCleery in Vancouver. Essayist, poet, 'gentle anarchist,' his final gift of verse was *The Cherry Tree on Cherry Street*, Quarry Press.